Transforming Through 2012

Leading Perspectives on the New Global Paradigm

Presented by Debra Giusti

Sponsored by
Paul and Lillie Weisbart—Stillpoint Now

Yinspire Media
info@yinspiremedia.com
www.YinspireMedia.com

Producer: Ruby Yeh

Presented by: Debra Giusti, Wishing Well Productions

Editorial Director: AJ Harper

Print Management: The Book Lab

Cover Design: Pearl Planet Designs

Book Design & Typesetting: Chinook Design, Inc.

ISBN-13: 978–0981970813

Printed in the United States of America

Contents

Contents

Contents

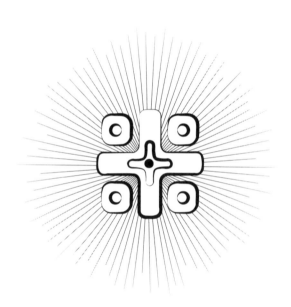

IN GRATITUDE...

I have deep appreciation for all the authors who contributed their time and resources to create this first book in the *Transforming Through 2012* series. I also honor the many hundreds of authors around the world who bring forth timely information on the 2012 topic, creating guideposts for this accelerated time.

I thank my producing team, each of whom saw the vision and invested their time, unique expertise and deep passion. They include: Tara Grace (Sponsor Liason/Author Research), Deborah Pozin (Resource Guide/Affiliate Relations), Mead Rose (Technical Manager), Tara Dewey (Author Research/Database Support), Deborah Pietsch (Marketing Director/Internet Strategist) and Lainie "Sevante" Quirk (Consultant/Sponsorships).

I am in deep appreciation for our presenting sponsor, the author team of Paul and Lillie Weisbart. Paul and Lillie are the inventors of the Scalar Wave Laser and the developers of Stillpoint Now, the space between the breath. Paul and Lillie share revolutionary new technology products and resources for healing and living an abundantly healthy life. Their work centers around the shift into the new season, and offers an easy process for dissolving stress, tension and dis-ease into the quantum neutral unified field state.

I thank all involved for offering the cutting edge products, movies, art and music found in the Resources for the New Paradigm Guide, available in the online multimedia version of Transforming Through 2012. Thank you to the filmmakers who created movies about the 2012 shift and the new paradigm such as: *Metaphysia 2012; Making the Quantum Leap; Hunab Ku; The Wiz Kidz; Return of the Ancestors,*

2012: Time for Change; Quantum Communication and *What on Earth?*
Many thanks to the musicians who composed music related to the
2012 shift. This group includes new paradigm artists who offer art/
music videos that speak directly to the spirit, and featured musician
Jonathan Goldman, who presents his "2012: Ascension Music."

I am in constant appreciation for my family, who always support
me with love and assistance so that I may manifest my visions as
gracefully as possible. They include my mother, Lorraine Giusti, who
has always stood by my side through all of my adventures growing
cutting edge businesses. I extend appreciation to my sister and
brother, Lori Todd and Paul Giusti, who constantly remind me that
I am blessed to have such strong family bonds. I give thanks to my
spiritual sister and brother, Elizabeth Moriarty and John Mitchell,
who help maintain my physical home and technological world.

I thank my publisher, Ruby Yeh, founder of Yinspire Media
and AliveEbooks, for paving the way with new technology. Her
revolutionary developments in publishing pioneered the online
multimedia ebook format that allows you, the reader, to continue the
2012 shift conversation through text, audio and video. Thank you to
the AliveEbooks team, Amber Ludwig (Author Liaison) and Sharon
Redmond (Multi-Media Coordinator).

Thank you to my editor, AJ Harper, founder of Book Lab, for
helping me manifest my vision for this book. And thank you to
the Book Lab team, Zoë Bird, Erik Simon and Kelly Andersson
(Editorial), Olaf Nelson (Interior Book Design) and Nicki Harper,
PhD (Editorial/Print Coordination).

I also thank Scott McKeown, Sean Ahearn, Bo Sapper, Leila
Rand, Lucretia Danner, Udi Kalig, Evalena Rose and the one Great
Spirit of All for supporting this creative process and my life.

Debra Giusti

WELCOME TO *TRANSFORMING THROUGH 2012*

I t is easy to see that we are living in rapidly evolving times. Never before have we had access to so much information and technology. We now have the ability to connect with and learn from great teachers—and one another—on a global scale. As we make this evolutionary leap, our knowledge grows, our understanding deepens and our vision expands, illuminating our vast potential and enabling a great paradigm shift. We are privileged to be on this planet at this time, positioned to witness and experience the outer (planetary and cultural) and inner (personal and spiritual) effects of this shift.

When I founded the Health & Harmony Festival in 1978, a new planetary consciousness was beginning to emerge in America. More than thirty years later, the (renamed) Harmony Festival is the largest event of its kind nationally, celebrating music, art, ecology, healthy living and spirituality. Every June in Santa Rosa, California, over thirty-five-thousand people collectively explore and manifest lifestyle changes that co-create health and harmony for all, and demonstrate the paradigm shift in action.

Over the years, as the festival expanded, so too did my awareness of our planet's accelerated transformation and the emerging 2012 shift. This new awareness has now made its way to the collective consciousness and the mainstream media, showing up in Hollywood movies, bestselling books and social networking. The topic of 2012 is now at the forefront of modern conversation.

> *We are privileged to be on this planet at this time, positioned to witness and experience the outer (planetary and cultural) and inner (personal and spiritual) effects of this shift.*

The many and varied predictions and opinions on the shift and 2012 have left some people feeling confused or frightened at the prospect of sweeping global, even *galactic,* changes. Personal or cultural change can be confusing, especially during a time when previous social, economic and environmental structures no longer serve. As these structures shift, making room for the new emerging potential, this is not the end of the world. It is the beginning of the next global paradigm. The need for clarity, truth and understanding about 2012 based on science, facts, prophecy and mystical teachings is available in our social and global culture. This is what you will receive through the *Transforming Through 2012* book series.

How do we answer the call to anchor new ways
of living and being?
How do we tune into higher guidance to find
safe and graceful pathways?
How do we move forward with ease
during these shifting times?

The *Transforming Through 2012* book series will offer the answers to these questions and more. This book provides a compass, sharing ways to navigate through these changing times. *Transforming Through 2012* is your "Resource Guide," empowering you to move beyond confusion and fear and to embrace the new opportunities and higher potential that will affect your day-to-day life and your future.

I've had the rare honor and privilege to meet, learn from and share dialogues with some of the most respected experts in the field of transformation—indigenous elders, mystics, healers, scientists, researchers, futurists, astrologers, artists and other luminaries, many of them contributors to this book. Authors such as noted scholar and visionary Jean Houston who explains "jump time," the period of "whole systems transition." Bestselling author and philosopher Daniel Pinchbeck shares his vision of a "new planetary culture based on communality of interest." Kymberlee Ruff, the "Messenger of the Hopi/Tibetan Prophecies," offers Grandfather Martin Gashweseoma's story of the "Two Paths of the Hopi Prophecy Rock."

> With the Transforming Through 2012 *series, I offer you a front-row seat to the global awakening.*

Other prominent authors include Paul and Lillie Weisbart, inventors of the Scalar Wave Laser and teachers of *Stillpoint* (the space between the breath), a systematic approach for transition into "the new season" and a gateway to the new quantum relativity; author and cellular biologist Bruce H. Lipton, an internationally recognized authority on bridging science and spirit and researcher Nassim Haramein, who developed a groundbreaking unification theory based on a new solution to Einstein's field equations. This book also includes articles written by indigenous elders representing traditions of the Maya, Hopi, Inca, Aztec and Hawaiian cultures.

With the *Transforming Through 2012* series, I offer you a front-row seat to the global awakening. *Transforming Through 2012* provides you with golden nuggets of valuable and timely information and insight, offering useful and practical tools for transformation while inspiring hope for our positive future. Each distinguished author provides a unique "leading perspective," yet all point to a similar conclusion: we are living in amazing, transformational times that offer untold possibilities for realizing our human potential.

And so our journey, *Transforming Through 2012*, begins.

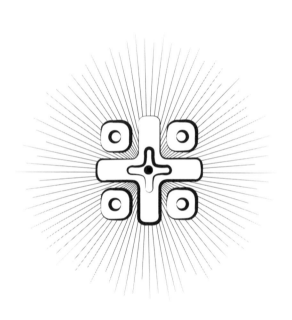

George Noory

FOREWORD

As December 21, 2012, draws near, its significance is the subject of increasing speculation. Every night, millions of listeners tune in to the nationally syndicated radio program *Coast to Coast AM* searching for answers to the big questions—why are we here? Where did we come from? Is there a grand plan for humankind, and if so, what's next?

As host of *Coast to Coast AM*, I know 2012 is a subject of great interest and concern. Over the past six years, I've interviewed various experts on 2012—scientists, historians, anthropologists, healers and others—some of whom are contributors to this book. While doomsayers mark 2012 as the end of the world, others look to it as the gateway to the next golden age. Whether one is optimistic, pessimistic or falls somewhere in between the two extremes, it is clear that change is upon us.

What we know for certain is that this date holds significance astronomically, astrologically and, particularly, as the ending date of the Mayan Long Count calendar. From a purely scientific perspective, it is a curious coincidence that our solar system crosses the galactic equator during the Winter Solstice of 2012. No big deal. Or is it?

There is geological evidence to suggest periodic reversals of the Earth's magnetic field, and some scientists believe that such reversals can be triggered by outside events—such as our solar system crossing the galactic equator. If any of this turns out to be true, then we may experience changes in our protective magnetosphere, which could result in increased solar radiation, particularly when we consider that this also coincides with a period of peak sunspot activity.

There is also geological evidence that Yellowstone National Park is actually a massive volcanic caldera one thousand times the size of Mount St. Helens, which erupts every six-hundred-forty-thousand years. We are overdue for another eruption, and some scientists speculate that geomagnetic changes could trigger it, resulting in volcanic ash covering large portions of the United States while simultaneously finding its way into the upper atmosphere, blocking sunlight and causing a new Ice Age. Add it all up and throw in some overactive plate tectonics, and it makes for a sensational modern-day retelling of Noah's Ark, as in the recent Sony Pictures movie, *2012*. Hurray for Hollywood!

> *Whether one is optimistic, pessimistic or falls*
> *somewhere in between the two extremes,*
> *it is clear that change is upon us.*

Finally, there is the possibility of the return of Planet X, or Nibiru, the theoretical brown dwarf binary partner of our sun, supposed home of the Annunaki master race. According to some calculations, its orbital period is 2,148 years, which would make us due for a visit in 2012. Nibiru has been blamed for Noah's flood; it perturbs planetary orbits and causes earthquakes and massive meteor showers as it passes through our solar system, drawing debris from the Oort cloud in its wake. Time will tell.

There are others who feel that the true significance of 2012 has more to do with the evolution of mankind in terms of a global shift in consciousness. For evidence they look to astrology, the Mayan Long Count calendar and eerily similar prophecies regarding 2012 from other ancient cultures.

Astrologically speaking, there is quite a bit going on around 2012. Probably the most significant occurrence has to do with the precession of the equinoxes, or the fact that where the sun rises at the equinox changes gradually over time. The period from 1988 to 2016 comprises a period of galactic alignment. Within this period it is predictable that on the December 21st solstice, the sun will rise at

> *Many interpret this Grand Alignment as the crossover point from a dark age into an age of accelerated evolution for mankind. Such an evolutionary shift is not without its challenges. People will be faced with the need to release old models and embrace entirely new ways of thinking, feeling and relating.*

the same point on the horizon as the bulge in the Milky Way, *exactly when we are crossing the galactic equator.* Astrologers refer to this as the "Grand Alignment," and interpretations of the meaning of this occurrence vary depending upon each astrologer and each method used. Many interpret this Grand Alignment as the crossover point from a dark age into an age of accelerated evolution for mankind. Such an evolutionary shift is not without its challenges. People will be faced with the need to release old models and embrace entirely new ways of thinking, feeling and relating.

Three other significant astrological occurrences to watch for at this time will be the transit of Venus (a harbinger of love and war), a total eclipse and a penumbral eclipse (both associated with natural disasters).

Researchers of indigenous peoples have noted a certain commonality among the prophecies of various elders, even in the most isolated tribes. This has led to speculation as to *why* there are similarities, and lends credibility to the notion that the ancestors of contemporary peoples were privy to knowledge that other cultures did not pass to their descendants. One can only guess as to the sources of such knowledge. Were the ancient peoples in possession of technology that was later lost? Was their extraordinarily accurate knowledge of astronomy and calendars imparted to them by extraterrestrials? Such questions are not as far-fetched as they might seem.

Transforming Through 2012: Leading Perspectives on the New Global Paradigm offers readers like yourself the unique opportunity to explore these questions, and others surrounding 2012, in one place. In this book, more than thirty experts, some of whom have been my guests on *Coast to Coast AM*, present a wide scope of perspectives on 2012 and the transforming planetary consciousness.

This book is an anthology of brilliant minds, looking into the future in an attempt to discern the course of humankind as we emerge from history into the next phase of our evolution. Consider the pages that follow to be both a primer on 2012, and a guidebook to help you navigate the great shift that is upon us. Turn to it for answers to *your* big questions.

The next phase promises to be an exciting ride with more than a few scares. I'm looking forward to these changes with anticipation.

Tata OmeAkaEhekatl Erick Gonzalez

STAY CLOSE TO THE FIRE

For generation after generation dating back to ancient times, the astronomers, mathematicians and scientists of the Maya and other Native American cultures have described a future event of cosmological, astronomical and planetary alignment that will have a profound effect on all life on Mother Earth: the end date of the 13 *Baktun* cycles on Dec 21, 2012. Having kept records of the Earth's historical clock and previous "stargate" alignments (i.e., global changes that mark the beginning and ending of eras in the past and mark the basis for similar calculations for the future), the Maya have prepared for this transition for thousands of years. A gathering of our entire human family, both indigenous and non-indigenous people, is necessary to see us through this great transition. No one should be left behind.

Many years ago, the Mayan elders of Guatemala asked me to share the message of the indigenous people of the world with the rest of our human relations—a message they have talked about (and a way of being they have lived) for thousands of years. In a small Guatemalan village in the mountains, way up in the cornfields, the elders asked me: "Can you bring our message to the people of the world?" It was a serious request. I was eighteen years old at the time I accepted this sacred responsibility, which became my path in life. From that time to this day, I've stayed close to our ceremonies, close to the sacred fire, and eventually became a spiritual leader and elder, an Aj Q'ij of the Mayan people. And in many forums and ceremonies held over the years in both the Americas and in other lands, I have tried to share their message.

As we live through the current prophesied transformation known as 2012, our sacred instructions from the elders—passed on through oral tradition—come down to this: "Stay close to the sacred fire and do not let it go out."

It is time to understand the changes that are occurring on our Mother Earth. This is a historical moment of great opportunity, a rare chance for humanity to undergo a conscious evolutionary process on many levels. It is a time to begin flowering in our living connection to nature and spirit so that together we can help to preserve life for future generations rather than destroy it as we are now doing. We must gather together in sacred ceremony and pass through the fire of transformation so that all life can make it through. It is time for us to awaken to the joyous transformation of humanity and take spiritual and practical responsibility for our future. We must begin to ask ourselves: What can we do now to transform ourselves so that the next seven generations can inherit a better world than the world we currently live in?

> *"Stay close to the sacred fire*
> *and do not let it go out."*

This great shift of humanity cannot happen in a merely intellectual way. It must happen in a spiritual, emotional way from a heartfelt and living connection to the elements. By bringing all our human relations to stand close to the fire in a ceremonial way, we can begin to form a new type of human being.

For the Maya and other indigenous societies, the sacred fire is the source of illumination through these challenging times. The sacred fire is a light to guide us through the darkness. And it is the source of celebration of oneness and wholeness not only with humanity but with all life, the Mother Earth and the cosmos. To stay close to the fire in its spiritual meaning is to keep our emotions positive and always moving towards love, harmony, oneness and light. Rekindling the spiritual and ceremonial fire within us transforms us into luminous beings. And through this fire we can prepare ourselves to pass through this coming cosmic alignment. We stay close to the ceremonial fire in order to remember spirit and keep the connection to spirit alive. When this relationship to spirit is strong, we can use this great cosmic shift to achieve a balanced and harmonious way of living on our Mother Earth.

This ceremonial fire, the first fire we have to connect with, begins as the fire in our hearts. The fire in our hearts we call love: love for ourselves, love for our families, love for all our relations, love for our Mother Earth, love for all that is given to us in creation. It begins with our connection to nature and leads us to experience great joy, wholeness, mental tranquility and an opening of the mind and heart necessary to co-create alternative and sustainable ways of living in the world today.

The next fire is the way we act on the physical plane, and this becomes our ceremonial fire, manifested physically during sacred ritual. When people stay close to this elemental fire, they can have divine experiences. They see reality for themselves and don't need anyone else to tell them what is sacred, who they are, how they should find their healing or what the Creator is. Their awareness becomes connected to the space they inhabit. They realize that whatever they do to the web of life, they do to themselves.

When we connect to the sacred fire in our hearts and to the elemental ceremonial fire, we engage in yet another ceremonial fire in the form of a pipe. Through the ritual of the pipe, we become participants with the fire, not by smoking tobacco or other substances, but by praying with medicines and connecting with life-giving Grandfather Fire, which is the Sun. From there, we learn that through the Sun (and the countless other suns that fill the sky) we can move through subtle dimensions, vortexes and universal portals known to the Maya and other indigenous people. The ancient Maya, for example, knew how to travel through thirteen different fires.

If we prepare in this way, we will be ready for the 2012 alignment known as 13 *Baktun*. On that day, our home, Mother Earth, will align with Grandfather Fire, our Sun, which will be aligned in turn with the central fires burning at the heart of our galaxy. For those who are ready, the heart fire will be aligned through the prayer in the pipe, through the healing ceremonial fire, through the life-giving fire of our Grandfather Sun, through the central fires that burn at the center of our galaxy—and beyond. No matter what is happening on the Earth, to the mind or to the body, stay close to the ceremonial fire.

Stay close to the elemental fire. Stay close to the fire in your heart. If you have ears to hear, the elemental fire will speak to you. It teaches and reveals. This fire does incredible things for us as human beings— not just burning or purifying, keeping us warm or preparing our food, but also gifting us with spiritual instruction. This is why, for the first time in history, the indigenous people are offering forums and bridges for non-indigenous people to participate in these sacred healing ceremonies.

> *No matter what is happening on the Earth, to the mind or to the body, stay close to the ceremonial fire. Stay close to the elemental fire. Stay close to the fire in your heart.*

Our instructions from the elders are to keep the sacred fire alive, for we have long known that humanity would someday need a place of refuge to reconnect with spirit. We believe that time is now.

For decades now, the indigenous spiritual leaders of the Americas have been preparing this refuge for humanity to gather together around the sacred fires. We are creating the spiritual containers, raising our ceremonial *malocas*, rebuilding our sacred *kivas*, activating our sweat lodges, rekindling our fires throughout our sacred cities and sacred sites and lighting the council fires of humanity inside the spiritual arbors of our people. We are opening our ceremonies to others and sharing our wisdom openly so that we can navigate collectively through this 2012 era by connecting with our inner fire. We must learn how to anchor our spiritual intentions and hold onto that vision during moments of intense transition and duality in the challenging times in which we now live.

> *To prevent the Earth's destruction, rather than waiting until it's already too late, the human family must reconnect through the spiritual trade routes.*

Long ago, the spiritual trade routes were the paths our people traveled throughout the Americas. Each nation traded its wisdom with other nations. And those who traded learned about the wider world and brought news and stories back to their people and shared them by acting out the stories around the communal fires. The Nations of the First Peoples of the Americas have continued to share their sacred fires—and to exchange wisdom as well as food and other goods we need to sustain us—down to the current time so that all our relations can celebrate and work together through whatever obstacles arise as we build a beautiful future for our children and the coming generations.

To prevent the Earth's destruction, rather than waiting until it's already too late, the human family must reconnect through the spiritual trade routes. At our sanctuary at Deer Mountain, and at similar sanctuaries throughout the Americas where we are gathering with the indigenous wisdom keepers of the Earth, we are re-establishing and traveling those spiritual trade routes today. We exchange tangible seeds to grow food and medicines and preserve the physical essentials needed to sustain us, but we also share seeds of story, ceremony, sustainability and survival, once again teaching each other the essential earth wisdom and traditions that survived the invasion from Europe. Sometimes we even cross dimensions to exchange what is sacred to us.

Today, our spiritual trade routes take us all over the world to connect our greater human families and share the sacred wisdom that each of these indigenous families holds so that all of us, together, can gather at the elemental fire. We must all act in integrity and open the circle of relations so that indigenous people can stand in their rightful place as the keepers of earth-medicine-wisdom and guide humanity through this great period of transformation in the years ahead.

———————

Tata Erick, also known by his Tolteca-Azteca name of OmeAkaEhekatl and the tribal name Ga'ada ("supernatural light"), which were given by his adopted Haida nation, is a lineage-holder and Daykeeper of the Cakchikel Maya of Guatemala. Tata Erick was ceremonially initiated as a Mayan Aj Q'ij ("staff of light") in 1994 and is a member of many indigenous councils throughout the Americas. He is a Daykeeper of the Mayan calendars and has trained in indigenous ceremonial ways for thirty-five years. Tata's ceremonies are held in accordance with the mathematics of the Chol Q'ij calendar of the Maya. The code of doctrine and discipline he uses is a reflection of the indigenous cosmological spirituality embedded in nature.

Tata Erick offers pre-recorded "Navigating 2012: Mayan Spiritual Teachings" and "Shamanic Spiritual Training" tele-seminars. For more information about Tata Erick's shamanic medicine teachings and events, sustainable communities and ceremonial healing centers in Guatemala and Deer Mountain (just north of Mt. Shasta in California), see the website for his not-for-profit organization, Tinamit Junan Uleu (Earth Peoples United), at www.EarthPeoplesUnited.org.

Jean Houston, PhD

THESE ARE THE TIMES; WE ARE THE PEOPLE

I use the term "jump time" to refer to what we sometimes call "punctuated equilibrium." When you look at the fossil record, you will see a species moving along, looking quite the same for a long time—and then, within a very short time, in terms of evolutionary perspective, there's a jump—and the species shifts and changes. These changes don't necessarily happen gradually, or over very long periods. I suggest that this is what is happening now to humanity. We have seen a series of jumps in the past, but probably never one as radical and far-reaching as the jump we are experiencing today.

This is probably the single most critical time in history, the time in which we make a decision whether to grow or die. Other people, in other times, believed that their time was it—they were wrong. *This* is it! So many different factors are coming together to really make what I call "whole system transition."

The problem is that most people have not been trained for whole system transition. They were trained for another era, in which things moved more slowly. Working with leaders all over the world, I find that many of them have been trained to be the equivalent of white males of the year 1926. They've not been trained for *this* extraordinary shift, in which we decide whether we grow or die. Part of my work is to prepare people for this shift—at all levels, from heads of state I've worked with to people who are pushing a broom.

To paraphrase Albert Einstein, the consciousness that created a problem cannot be the same consciousness that solves it. My work for many years has been in human development. Now, working with the United Nations and other international agencies, my task is to help prepare people to use more of their minds, bodies, spirits and energies in a consummate ecology of use of their own inner spaces and capacities—in the light of social change. We suffer from a gross overuse of the outer world, and a horrendous underuse of the inner world. This is where so many of our problems arise.

> *I suggest that this is what is happening now to humanity. We have seen a series of jumps in the past, but probably never one as radical and far-reaching as the jump we are experiencing today.*

The whole notion of 2012 is very interesting. I've read the literature, and I know José Argüelles, who's an extraordinary, brilliant, wildly radical, and innovative thinker. The connection of Mayan prophecies and the Mayan calendar with the precession of the equinox and the shifting of the ages is fascinating. My own take on it is that we have *been* in this extraordinary time now for some years. It is in the nature of the linear Christian calendar, especially, to focus on a special time when the Messiah comes. We evolve, we reach a certain point, and then the great event happens—the heavens open up and the redemption occurs. This is a very strong theme in Western culture. So naturally, the whole notion of 2012 really pops into some minds and says, "This is it! This is the redeeming event." It's a very ancient way of perceiving history and time.

But I don't think this time is about redemption. I think it is about evolution. What we're being asked to do is to grow in the amplitude of our spirit, our being, in the utilization of the incredible resources of our body, mind and spirit, in our ability to cross the great divide of otherness and really speak to each other in unique and powerful ways. I think that people are focusing on the notion of 2012 because it gives us a sense of specific space and time, an event around which we can gather resources and begin to become adequate stewards of biological and social evolution—stewards of our planet and of ourselves.

We're being asked to recognize and develop our innate capacities, and bring them to bear upon the great issues of our times. The most important capacity to develop is the sense that you *are* important in this time, that you are not an encapsulated bag of skin dragging around a dreary little ego, but an organism at one with both the world and the changing times. With that sense, you release a lot of old holding patterns and obstructions. You begin to realize that you have capacities that you didn't know you had, or that you may have had as a child and then lost—capacities for creative imagination, and for many different ways of thinking: thinking in images; thinking with words; thinking kinesthetically with the whole body; thinking from the heart. And when you bring this extraordinary reservoir of capacities to yourself and the world, you find ways of crossing the great divide of otherness. You are able to work in teams in much more fluent, flexible and creative ways. You make things happen. But it really starts from the inside out, not from outside in, as we in the West have been taught; creativity is alive beneath the surface crust of consciousness all the time.

> *We're being asked to recognize and develop our innate capacities, and bring them to bear upon the great issues of our times.*

I've had the good fortune to study, in person, fifty-five of the most creative individuals in North America, extraordinary people such as Margaret Mead, Buckminster Fuller and Joseph Campbell, the great mythologist whom I knew and worked with for twenty years. I found that these folks were archaeologists of their own minds, spelunkers in the caves of their own creativity. Thus, they had the inner hooks and eyes, the inner images, feeling states and abilities to grasp a creative idea as it evolved and emerged. They gave the passion to the possible to do something about it. Thinking in images—not just visual images, but auditory and kinesthetic images too—gives one the neuronal enthusiasm to leap to an extraordinary level of creativity. I find that people who think in images are able to do more and think faster. The mind in this state of heightened creativity races, selects, synthesizes and sometimes does the work of months in moments. We need to tap into these capacities in order to become the humans this era requires.

> *We have been living in mythic times for some time now, and a great deal is being required of us.*

We're living in a time where time itself is in a wild acceleration. How do you live, psychologically, in a jump time, where everything is changing constantly? I show people how to take on many different modalities of time, even what we would call subjective time, when one can experience in minutes what sometimes would be hours or days. There are parts of the mind that do not know time. And the brain is not hardwired, as we previously thought. On the contrary, it has remarkable capacities for reorganizing and regrowing itself.

People like Bruce Lipton are showing that thinking, learning, acting, intending (that's a *big* one), meditating and enjoying can activate the basic genetic structures of our bodies and minds so we can not only shape our own brain anatomy and behavior—we can literally grow new capacities. I believe from many years of research, we can even grow new, evolved human versions of ourselves. This is a great cause for hope and action in this critical time.

A myth is something that never was but is always happening. Myth is, I believe, the proto-DNA of the human psyche. My old friend Joe Campbell believed that it was coded in the body, and I suspect that this is true, because a myth functions by serving as the lure of becoming. It gives you a basic story template, out of which you can begin to take on the larger sense of who you are, where you are, what you yet can be. We have been living in mythic times for some time now, and a great deal is being required of us.

We are mythic beings, embarking continually on journeys of growth and discovery. The whole notion of 2012 is an image around which our time's requirements are traveling like planets around the sun. And if the idea of 2012 is making people grow up and be responsible, then great. Hegel once wrote about world-historical individuals, people whose passion corresponded to the turning of their time, that whether they were out front or behind the scenes, they became the entrepreneurs of progress. They did a lot of work on themselves to be relevant, resonant and ready for the great challenges of their times.

That's what we need to do to meet this extraordinary jump time. I don't personally believe that any horrible thing is going to happen. But I do think that if people can use the year 2012 as a point to grow themselves into ready stewards of this planetary process, let's not hold back.

Jean Houston, PhD, scholar, philosopher and researcher in human capacities, is one of the foremost visionary thinkers and doers of our time. She is regarded as one of the principal founders of the Human Potential Movement. In 1965, along with her husband Dr. Robert Masters, she founded The Foundation for Mind Research. She is also the founder and principal teacher of the Mystery School, a program of cross-cultural, mythic and spiritual studies dedicated to teaching history, philosophy, the new physics, psychology, anthropology, myth and the many dimensions of human potential.

Dr. Houston is a prolific writer and author of twenty-six published books, including A Passion for the Possible, The Possible Human *and* A Mythic Life: Learning to Live Our Greater Story. *Her book* Jump Time *explores a new global paradigm and speaks boldly of a re-genesis of human society. The questions raised in this book and the exciting suggestions of possibilities are producing new pioneers—social artists—working on the frontiers of this new global society. Dr. Houston also offers seminars in social artistry. A powerful and dynamic speaker, she holds conferences and seminars with social leaders, educational institutions and business organizations worldwide. Dr. Houston has worked in over one-hundred countries and is the recipient of many awards. She works at all levels of leadership and is currently broadening her work with the United Nations as a Senior Advisor to the UNDP—training leaders in developing countries in this new field of social artistry (human development in the light of social complexity). In 2007, Dr. Houston received a mandate from Dr. Monica Sharma, the Director of Leadership and Capacity Development for the UN, to train ten-thousand trainers, who in turn will be training some one-hundred-million people worldwide by 2017.*

Jean Houston's ability to inspire and invigorate people enables her to readily convey her vision—the finest possible achievement of the individual potential—while sharing with her audiences and students the inner fire and excitement of that possibility! Visit www. JeanHouston.com

John L. Petersen

A NEW END: A NEW BEGINNING

I've been thinking about the possibility of large-scale change for quite some time. (My wife would probably tell you that I think about it all of the time.) I generally agree with the many thoughtful people who consider predicting the future to be a fool's errand. It is intrinsically fraught with so much complexity and uncertainty that the best one can do with integrity is to array potential alternatives—scenarios—across the horizon, and then try to think about what might be done if one of those worlds materializes.

Scenario-planning has certainly been an effective discipline, helping many organizations to imagine potentialities that probably otherwise wouldn't have shown up in their field of view. But as I facilitate organizations going through these exercises, the little, nagging voice in the back of my head is not asking, "What is the array of possible futures?" It is always wondering, "What is the future *really* going to be?"

No one knows for sure what the future will bring, but after being in this business for some time, one begins to be able to discriminate between what is substantive and structural and what is largely speculative. For me, at least, some things have an intuitive sense of being real and important, and the rest of the possibilities lack just enough gravitas to indicate to me that they're only "ideas." That intuitive sense is supported when it becomes possible to triangulate from a number of independent sources that all point to the same conclusion—the possibility has substance.

People always ask me what I think is going to happen. "With all of these converging trends, what is 2012 really going to look like?" It happened again last week in a radio interview. Mostly I hedge and dance a bit and say that I don't know for sure. But, over a year ago, the notion that all of this big change could spell the substantial reconfiguration of the familiar country that I have lived in all of my life began to gel in a way that moved beyond the notion of being just a possibility—a wild card—and into that space of plausibility. I have now come to believe that it is likely and will happen—soon. There are numerous indicators that suggest the big change is coming.

> *There are numerous indicators that suggest the big change is coming.*

Multiple trends are converging. Huge, extraordinary, global trends, any number of which would be enough to derail our present way of life, are converging to precipitate a historic, big transition event. A partial list would include: the collapse of the global financial system, the end of petroleum, increased irregularities in local climates, global food shortages and the effects of larger solar eruptions on communications.

Problems are much larger than government. These kinds of problems are much greater than anything that contemporary governments have ever had to deal with. Peak oil, climate change and the financial meltdown by themselves have the potential to significantly overwhelm the capabilities of government. If these extraordinary, disruptive events end up being concurrent, then the whole system is at risk.

The problems are structural. They're systemic. Some of these issues, especially the financial, oil and food problems, are also a product of how we live, our priorities and our paradigms. We are

14

creating the problems because of our values and principles. Without extraordinary, fundamental changes in the way we see ourselves and the world, we will keep getting what we are getting.

Leaders think the old system can be "rebooted." Almost everyone in leadership positions in the US, and in other countries, wants to make the old system well again. That is why:

We're not dealing with the structural issues. All of the biggest efforts are attempts to re-inflate the financial bubble, and keep the mortally wounded institutions alive. The knee-jerk reactions come from the same people who helped to design and feed the present system. These people are also deluded—they think (or act like) they know what they are doing. They don't realize that:

The situation is so complex that no one really understands it. The Global Business Network's Peter Schwartz, reporting on a conversation with Martin Wolff of the *Financial Times*, said that Wolff's key point was that the nature and scale of the credit crisis is so novel that it's not clear we know what we're doing when we try to stop it. He is deeply worried. We are in uncharted waters.

The issues are global. Japan's exports fell by forty-six percent in January of 2009. In the last eight months, sixty-five-thousand factories closed in China, which means products aren't being shipped.

The system is fundamentally out of balance. In the US, the rich are getting richer (at unconscionable rates). National media has reported that the government is monitoring all internal communications of its citizens—but it lies and says it is not. Common sense is not included in big, sweeping federal edicts. For example, it's also now against the law in some states, like Illinois, for farmers to save the seeds that they've grown—they must buy new ones each year from large seed companies.

Most of the US federal budget goes to the military. More than half of the US federal budget goes to military and military-related agencies. This kind of growth, of course, is what brought down the Soviet Union. In sharp contrast to the political apparatchiks who protest that more money is needed to reverse the shrinking, aging and decline in readiness of the Army, Navy and Air Force, few seem to understand that budget increases are a primary cause of the problems.

No new ideas, government can't be responsive. They're in charge, but they have no new ideas for solutions to these massive issues. They're also slow—and this situation needs fast, agile responses. There is an additional problem: even if they did have good ideas, the government wouldn't be able to effectively implement them because:

Too many lawyers and lobbyists cause too much inertia. There is a huge, well-funded effort in place to maintain the status quo or to shift the future to benefit one group at the expense of others. It would be impossible within the present system to initiate dramatic change when the threat was still on the horizon. Only when the crisis was about to crash down on everyone—when adequate time and resources for effective response were nonexistent—might everyone pull together for the common good.

> *Only when the crisis was about to crash down on everyone—when adequate time and resources for effective response were nonexistent—might everyone pull together for the common good.*

Potential solutions take too long to implement. These issues are so gigantic that confronting and redirecting them takes a long time. We do not operate with either that foresight or resolve.

Supply chains are long and thin. Globalism and just-in-time production has produced supply chains in most areas of commerce that are very long—often to the other side of the Earth—and very fragile. There are many places between there and here where something can go wrong.

$600 trillion in derivatives makes a house of cards. Looming over the whole financial situation is an almost unfathomable quantity of financial instruments—derivatives—which are essentially casino bets with no underlying value supporting the transaction. Warren Buffett calls them financial weapons of mass destruction that could bring the whole system down.

Cooperation is unlikely, protectionism will prevail. Instead of countries cooperating with each other to deal with these big transnational problems, we're seeing a pulling back to protect each country's perceived short-term interests, regardless of what the implications might be in the longer term.

> *Here's the catch. This might not happen.*

History says it's time. Perhaps what is most compelling to me is that history strongly suggests that the time is right for an upset. I talk about this in my book a bit, but the short version is that big punctuations in the equilibrium of evolution have produced extraordinary, fundamental reorganizations to life on this planet on a regular, accelerating basis since the beginning of time as we know it.

So, it doesn't look to me like we're going to be able to do what might be needed to maintain the present system...and it is likely that we're at one of those extraordinary moments in history when each of us gets the opportunity to play an important role in not only transitioning to a new world, but also designing it.

Here's the catch. This might not happen. There are any number of reasons why this scenario might not manifest itself, not least of which is that there will be many thousands, if not millions, of people who will be working very hard to assure that the system doesn't come apart (but then, they may be doing the wrong things). Seems to me, therefore, that flexibility and permeability (allowing new ideas to get through) are of critical importance here. Remember the first law of Discordianism: "Convictions cause convicts." Whatever you believe imprisons you.

So, stay loose. The winners need to transcend, not try to work their way through all of this. Don't get emotionally involved in the reports of the current global erosion. Concentrate on building the new world.

—————————

John L. Petersen is considered by many to be one of the most informed futurists in the world. He is best known for writing and thinking about high-impact surprises—wild cards—and the process of surprise anticipation. In 1989 John founded The Arlington Institute (TAI), a non-profit, future-oriented research institute. The "think tank" serves as a global agent for change by developing new concepts, processes and tools for anticipating the future and translating that knowledge into better present-day decisions.

His first book, The Road to 2015: Profiles of the Future, *was awarded Outstanding Academic Book of 1995 by CHOICE Academic Review, and remained on The World Future Society's (WFS) bestseller list for more than a year. John's latest book,* Out of the Blue: How to Anticipate Wild Cards and Big Future Surprises, *was also a WFS bestseller. His current book,* A Vision for 2012: Planning for Extraordinary Change, *presents practical ways in which individuals and organizations can deal with very large-scale change.*

A provocative public speaker, he addresses a wide array of audiences around the world on a variety of futurist subjects. When he is not writing or speaking, theorizing about wild cards or constructing his own airplane, John leads workshops that help corporate clients build new images of possible futures and visions for reaching their goals. He lives in the eastern panhandle of West Virginia with his wife, Diane. To learn more about John visit www.ArlingtonInstitute.org.

Barbara Marx Hubbard

BECOMING A
UNIVERSAL SPECIES

Every personal crisis is an opportunity to change, to grow, to
evolve. We all face crises. We have deaths in our families; friends
become ill; we may lose our jobs. Each of these crises is necessary to
jolt us from our daily routine, our planned path, and give us the
chance to move to a new level.

Every crisis a species faces is, similarly, an opportunity to evolve.
Our species was faced with a crisis millions of years ago when our
ancestors' environment changed from forest to grassland. Our
ancestors took the evolutionary leap and learned to walk on two
legs. This freed hands for tool use, and that resulted in larger, better
brains. As we approach 2012, humanity faces crises related to global
warming and climate change, world economic systems, nuclear
arms—and the list grows.

The great difference here is that we are the first species that knows
it is facing crises of its own making that could render us extinct or
empower us to evolve. This awareness marks the beginning of the
first age of conscious evolution. We belong to the first generations
to face crises that could destroy our own biosphere. As a species, we
have faced that possibility since the development of the atomic bomb.
But at the same time, many millions of people are waking up, asking,
"What can I do?" The answer does not lie with old governmental
systems or educational institutions, nor with religions, but with

innovation and creativity in every field. As the danger accelerates, innovation grows.

The crises now converging can bring an end to the dominator culture—with its over-population, separate-mindedness, environmental abuse and weapons of mass destruction—as our species makes its first conscious leap to our next phase. We have been told that we are at a bifurcation point, where the human species can either go down to further collapse, or make a positive shift through collaboration and connectivity. It depends on what *we* do. We are at a "chaos window." The system is out of balance. It can not continue by doing more of the same. We must innovate and transform, or we will devolve and self destruct. And there isn't much time to make this choice.

> *As the danger accelerates, innovation grows.*

The key to our possible rapid evolution is to connect what is working in every field and function toward a sustainable and evolvable world. It is to learn "social synergy" through collaboration and co-creativity. The very effort to connect the positive will evolve us toward the next phase of our species. We could become a "universal humanity," capable of co-evolving with nature and co-creating with Spirit. Our conscious evolution is being accelerated by the non-linear, exponential connectivity of what is emerging, through social networks of all kinds, driven by sacred activism—that is, action from the heart for the common good.

I believe that, by 2012, we can share together a "planetary birth experience," the awareness that we are one planetary body with the technology, resources and know-how to make it through these crises together. Already we see enough innovations in technology, in health—in every sector—to give pioneering souls the vision of our birth as a universal species. Such innovations are breaking through in every area, but they are not visible in the media, or in our mainstream politics. You can see them with "evolutionary eyes," that notice what is breaking through out of what is breaking down.

Our new capacities, especially in science and technology, make our next evolutionary leap very different from past changes. The next stage will be born not from random selection and survival of the fittest, but from the conscious choice of creative people working in synergy, integrating and applying our spiritual, social and scientific capacities. Technologically, we're gaining the powers once attributed to gods. Advances such as biotechnology, nano-technology, robotics, artificial intelligence and worldwide communication through the Internet put us on the threshold of no longer being creature humans. We are going to be co-creative humans, universal humans, and I think eventually we will be a universal species on this Earth, in the solar system, and in the galaxy.

> We are going to be co-creative humans, universal humans, and I think eventually we will be a universal species on this Earth, in the solar system, and in the galaxy.

Our spiritual capacities are ancient, but in the past people projected their own innate abilities onto gods, masters or institutions. Now, millions of us are now feeling the spirit *within ourselves*, becoming spiritually activated: co-creative humans. We are bringing the gods home as our own evolutionary potential.

We can appreciate our challenges without judgment. In the social realm, no one has ever before been asked to evolve a planet. There are no experts. Nobody on this Earth has seen a co-evolutionary, co-creative society. We are being asked to divine the design of social evolution—to design a world.

What is forming right now is a worldwide community of pioneering souls, a communion of people attracted to expressing and giving their gifts to the world. When we meet each other there is an instant rapport. The connectivity of such evolving humans is rapidly creating a resonant field, and a new critical mass of coherence and creativity that can shift the direction of human history.

As we probe into matter we find, through quantum physics, that there *is* no matter, that underneath energy there is a field, and underneath the field there seems to be an ordering process. It looks as though the most advanced scientific research is in tapping into the mind of the cosmos—seeking to understand the way consciousness itself creates.

> *The greater the emergency, the faster the emergence. The situation itself is empowering.*

I am a proponent and practitioner of sacred activism, the sacred part of conscious evolution. When I ran for the Vice Presidential nomination in 1984, I proposed a Peace Room that would identify the work of sacred activists. It would scan for and map connections and communicate what is working in the world to mobilize for constructive action. This is beginning to happen now. The Foundation for Conscious Evolution is working in collaboration with others to bring the Peace Room, now called the Synergy Engine, into reality. The worldwide web, which was in its infancy in 1984, gives us the tools to scan for what's emerging and bring people with ideas together. Scaled-up synergy and fast connections will let us show people how to apply conscious evolution in their own lives, for their own benefit, and for the greatest good of their neighbors and all of humanity.

The greater the emergency, the faster the emergence. The situation itself is empowering. The new society will involve people who see common goals and then match their talents with the needs of others. While we are increasing global intelligence by making creative ideas available for synergistic cooperation, we will also re-localize, as each person gives their gifts where they are needed.

We have the most wonderful opportunity humanity has ever faced. Without crisis, humanity would not make the leap to evolve into a new culture. As a species, we would remain in our fairly comfortable rut, fearing the unknown effects of change. The crises surrounding 2012 force us to change our society and ourselves. The new social structures we consciously create will not encourage survival of the fittest, in the old evolutionary paradigm. Rather they will free each of us to make our own unique contributions. It will be what Jonas Salk called "the survival of what fits best."

As a global society, we will experience more synergy, as people with varied skills make vital connections. But that society will also be localized, as people share the results of that synergy where they are most needed. I envision local synergy centers, so people can connect with one another where they live and act based on local needs. These centers would help people develop alternative currencies to empower them to go beyond over-monetization to support collaboration and co-creativity.

It is important for us to share our visions of a universal humanity. This much we can already see: If humanity succeeds in moving to the next evolutionary stage, we will have expanded, and extended, intelligence. As members of one living planetary body, we will have matured into a consciousness of the whole system. We will have longer life spans. We will have powers we once projected onto gods, but those powers will be our own.

We will restore the Earth, free ourselves from deficiencies, develop synergistic social systems, release untapped human potential, inhabit the solar system and eventually become galactic humans. We will be born as universal persons.

A noted futurist, author, social architect and speaker, Barbara Marx Hubbard is a founding board member of the World Future Society and co-founded the Foundation for Conscious Evolution. Barbara is the producer and narrator of the award-winning DVD series "Humanity Ascending: A New Way Through Together." She's written five books: The Hunger of Eve; The Evolutionary Journey; Revelation: Our Crisis Is a Birth; Conscious Evolution: Awakening the Power of Our Social Potential *and* Emergence: The Shift from Ego to Essence, Ten Steps to the Universal Human.

Barbara earned a BA in political science at Bryn Mawr College and studied at L'Ecole des Sciences Politique and the Sorbonne. She earned the first Doctor of Conscious Evolution degree awarded by the Emerson Theological Institute. She currently lives in Santa Barbara, California. To learn more about Barbara, visit www.BarbaraMarxHubbard.com.

Rev. M. Kalani Souza

ARISE, AWAKEN

E ala e　　　　　　　　Arise, awaken
ka La i ka hikina　　　　the Sun is in the east
i ka moana　　　　　　beyond the deep ocean
ka moana hohonu,　　beyond even the curved horizon
pi'i ka lewa　　　　　of the ocean, it climbs in space
ka lewa nu'u　　　　　in space till it reaches the zenith
i ka hikina　　　　　　there in the east
aia ka La　　　　　　　there is the Sun
e ala e.　　　　　　　　this is the way of it.
　　—*Edith Kanaka'ole*

This is the way of it. Every day the sun rises in the East. And every day that you are alive, you face the rich array of life experiences that lie directly in front of you. For more than a millennium, Polynesians, Micronesians and all other peoples of Oceania have lived and developed the science of survival by being present to the moment, alive in each breath. They have survived by simply observing what is, not by getting caught up in projections two months or two years down the line.

Whether the present day offers seemingly pleasurable or fearful experiences, it is wise to observe and evaluate where you are today and what you want your next step to be. Only then can you readjust your actions to allow for the best chance of survival to the next sunrise. Those who failed this critical criterion did not live to tell any tales, or to influence the stories of succeeding generations.

Recently, I was asked to address President Obama's Interagency Ocean Policy Task Force regarding "Indigenous Perspectives on Science and Conservation." They set an impossible task. I was given five minutes to distill the experience of all native populations of the Pacific, regarding a resource as all-encompassing as "the Ocean." Yet I would rather fail in the attempt than not attempt it at all. Such is my nature, and such are the circumstances I find myself in yet again as I attempt to write this chapter. These words I have written will not be true for all. However, these words will be true for myself, Kalani, *e ala e.*

> *These are not resources; these are relatives. These are relatives and we are always in relationship.*

In most instances, the "culture of tradition" and the "culture of modernity" have commonalities; they are both deeply rooted in a greater experience we can call the "meta-culture" of humanity. The culture of the traditional, of indigenous persons, is arguably that of the surviving socio-civilizations and tribal affiliations pre-Industrial Revolution, and reflects the first ten-thousand years of human experience; the culture of modernity is one arguably developed in Europe, then exported or colonized throughout the world during the last six centuries. The divergence in our current experience occurs way upstream in the cultural river. It affects how we see our place in the environment, for example. Modernity refers to the environment in terms like "natural resources;" tradition or my grandfather asks, "Does this tree dream of being your chair?" These are not resources; these are relatives. These are relatives and we are always in relationship.

Imagine, if you will, an ancient civilization: commerce, trade in Oceania and, in an expansion mode along the edges of Oceania's frontier outreaches, a family group. Beyond the far horizon, this group lives on some isolated islands, islands today known as Hawaii. For some four hundred years, these people live rigorous and peaceful lives, lives of plenty with little to no conflict (as is the case when needs are met). The population increases, stresses mount, food capacity and the social constructs that afford sustainable balance develop. Cultural norms, religious practices and civilization develop around watershed and family needs. Family culture and the culture of fishermen and farmers dominate, as in most Polynesian societies, and the initial migrants, though likely from many varied locations, create a new prosperous civilization together.

In this new civilization, a fledgling class of soothsayers and omen- and sky-watchers prophesy the coming of war, conflict and a change to life as they know it. Soon, journeyers from the far South begin to arrive, bringing with them a warrior culture that spreads over the previously peaceful collective—eventually dominating, and overlaying new cultural norms. The newcomers impose a caste system; their chiefs and aristocracy rule over a servant class of farmers and fishers.

Out of this oppressed social construct arose new religions, and prophets who predicted the arrival of the "bright eyes." These were foreigners, strangers with different ways, who would bring about the downfall of the warrior king's families. It was said that within a few generations, the foreigners would change the world as they knew it, returning control to the *makaainana* (the commoners) and re-establishing social status and governance by those who are close to nature and to the natural processes that produce food. And still, it is about relationships.

As we approach 2012, we find ourselves at yet another turn on the wheel, a potential shift in the human experience. It is as if the collective human race is holding its breath, somehow unconsciously aware of the potential for great change. This is a time for new thinking. I say, let us do this re-imagining consciously, fearlessly expressing our desire to grow as a global community, as the human race. Let us innovate and adapt new practices in commerce, in behavior and in community capacity.

Let us consciously begin a de-urbanization of the human experience, returning to more natural, rural, environmentally friendly settings and living areas to experience our place in nature in relationship to the environment and more closely akin to our ancestors. We need responsible, adaptive practices, rooted in good

> *Let us consciously begin a de-urbanization of the human experience, returning to more natural, rural, environmentally friendly settings and living areas to experience our place in nature in relationship to the environment and more closely akin to our ancestors.*

science but not devoid of critical spiritual evaluation as it feeds the need of mankind. The moment of great change is upon us. Truly, the time of the *mahi'ai*, the farmer, is again upon us. The choice is upon us, too, to merge the ancient ways with the advances of modern technology. We can choose to plant our food, to engage in the sacred hunt, to move intentionally back into active relationship with the environment of which we are a part—and at one with.

The past is in the future; the future is in the past. The Polynesians kept rhythm with the moon, the grandmother who protects the Mother Earth. How does this compare to a culture like the Maya, who ardently track their solar relationship, in the lesser and greater cycles of life? What does the date December 21, 2012, mean for Polynesians? What can I share that has been told to me regarding that specific date? I can share that the moon will be in its growing phase, the night of *'ole kulua*, a night not favored by those who plant, nor by those who go down to the sea. I can share values, values that I am re-teaching and re-affirming, values that may bolster us through these changing times. I can share some insights gathered at the "feet" of elders, speak of shared conversations, of writings, of songs and poems that tease and play out their messaging and grow in ways unexpected and greatly loved, of a voice that gives rise to the wealth of wisdom available to all Polynesians. A gentle, compassionate and connected people they are, *e ala e.*

> *No life without death, no joy without loss, no fear without courage, no dream without awakening,* e ala e.

Pono: Balance. To know the paradox, to see it in all you perceive. We need to maintain an inclusive perspective of the paradox, day to night, shadow to light, masculine to feminine, yin to yang. My father said, "If you cannot see the hundred-eighty-degree view from that which you perceive, then what you are observing is illusion." This is a simple gift he gave me, a simple test by which to push back on our beliefs. The mechanistic universe, the measurable, empirical, scientific view of the universe exists alongside the mystery, the divine, the spiritual, the indescribable—and both hold equal sway over our experience. No life without death, no joy without loss, no fear without courage, no dream without awakening, *e ala e.*

Lokahi: Harmony, for harmony's sake. To seamlessly integrate, to attune to all. First, *lokahi is* to be in harmony with the cosmos, to sense one's place in the whole of experience. Second, it is to be in harmony with the environment, with nature, with the nurturance in which we exist, and to feel ourselves a part of the source of our sustenance, to relate to our surroundings. Third, it is to be in harmony with our fellow man, to join in community as family connected through ritual and rite to the intergenerational strength of purpose. The last and perhaps most important lesson is to be in harmony with oneself. To harmoniously create a capacity in our societies and educational institutions that fosters the deep work of self-exploration and self-identification around purpose, competence and compassion, *e ala e.*

Malama: To care for, to sustain, to be mutually sustainable, to serve as you are served, to give back in full measure what you have extracted, freely. To know deeply that all your actions, decisions and thoughts affect all of experience. To know that you are significant in all that occurs and yet no more significant than all else. And we find ourselves back at the paradox, *mai pono, e ala e.*

These are just some of the great truths that indigenous people have to offer the world. But I ask you, who among us is not indigenous to this Earth? Indigenous knowledge is simply truth found when attending to our delicate relationship with all that surrounds us. Sitting in quiet observation of the world, and attending to the present moment with wisdom and insight, is all that you need to connect to this truth. This is just another chapter in the story of the human race: its relationship to all and in particular its relationship to itself. Wisdom is a thing that can be learned, but cannot be taught. We have much to learn, *e ala e.*

Rev. M. Kalani Souza is a gifted storyteller, singer, songwriter, musician, performer, poet, philosopher, priest, political satirist and peacemaker. Born in Honolulu, Hawai'i, Kalani began traveling abroad at sixteen, exploring humankind in its natural setting. His native roots allow him a unique perspective of the collision of two worlds—one steeped in traditional culture, the other a juggernaut of new morality and changing economic and political persuasion. A cross-cultural facilitator and lecturer, Kalani promotes social justice through conflict resolution in workshops nationwide and in Europe. His workshops and lectures inspire, challenge and entertain listeners while calling all to be their greater selves.

Kalani taught for and served on the Committee for Intense Public Conflict of the Association for Conflict Resolution (ACR). He serves as the chairman of Indigenous Knowledge Hui of the Pacific Risk Management Ohana, a collection of federal, state, county and non-governmental agencies working primarily to mitigate and respond to disasters in the greater Pacific region. He also serves as a cultural competency consultant for the National Oceanic and Atmospheric Administration (NOAA) Pacific Services Center of the Department of Commerce, and previously served as one of two Hawaiians in the Native Network, a group of four-hundred-fifty peacemakers in the Department of the Interior's Morris Udall Center for Peace in Tucson, Arizona. Kalani is a mentor with the Hawaiian non-killing effort of the Spark Matsunaga Center for Peace and is on the board of the Ala Kahakai Trail Association. He is also the Executive Director of the Olohana Foundation, a not-for-profit focused on community capacity. He currently resides on the island of Hawai'i. Watch Kalani's video message at www.1000VoicesArchive.org or visit his website, www.mkalani.com.

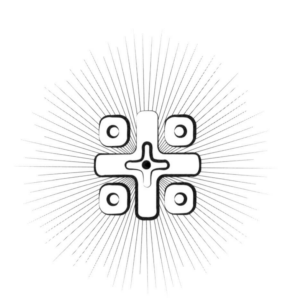

Paul and Lillie Weisbart

STILLPOINT: THE SPACE BETWEEN THE BREATH

Take a nice deep breath in. As you slowly let it out, relax and dissolve into the space between the breath. This is *stillpoint*, the space between the breath. In this stillpoint state, there is a vast reservoir of universal energy that can help clear and dissolve injuries, stress tension, dis-ease and cellular memory. Stillpoint is a gateway into the unified field state and quantum consciousness.

Yogis live in stillpoint. Their experience on this planet is very different from that of most people. Their breathing and brain waves are different; they are able to access the unique compounds in the glands that activate higher states of consciousness and open them to amazing untapped potentials for which the human body is naturally keyed and designed.

2012 is our planet going into stillpoint. As the Earth and its star system approach alignment with the galactic center of the universe, we all have the incredible opportunity to connect with the neutral unified field state in the same way yogis, mystics and shamans do. As we enter into this stillpoint state, our bodies naturally dissolve stress, tension and dis-ease and open to the quantum biological process that activates the glands and subtle body, flowering us into cosmic consciousness and the full expression of who we really are.

We are on the edge of a new season, a unique moment ancient cultures and mystics refer to as the "shift of the ages." This new season dawns as we move through the twenty-six-thousand-year cycle mapped out by the Maya. In the same way that there are seasons that govern our cycles here on Earth, there are much larger cycles or seasons that govern the astrological and cosmological physics of our star's transit through the universe. The Maya understood this, and mapped these cycles to navigate the shift and transition here. In the new season, we have the opportunity to collectively manifest systems and situations that reflect who we really are: conscious beings, connected to the universe, filled with all its wonders.

2012 is our planet going into stillpoint.

The Mayan cycle is the exact same twenty-six-thousand-year cycle that science calls the axial precession. Axial precession refers to the change in a planet's rotational axis. Imagine a top spinning very fast. As it slows down, it starts to wobble as the axis toward the top moves between two different points. This movement is polarity. When the top comes to a perfect point in the middle, all polarity dissolves. This is neutrality. The reality is that there are only two things going on in the universe: polarity and neutrality. The yogis call this karma and universal energy. If our planet were a top, it would take twenty-six-thousand years to complete its spin cycle. We are coming to the end of one cycle and the beginning of another, approaching a plum line where everything lines up perfectly and all of the different experiences to the sides of the true alignment dissolve. When our planet comes to a perfect point in 2012, we will experience neutrality. This is stillpoint.

So everything in the galaxy is spinning through this range of polarity. The galaxy is a big spiral, and what makes a spiral is the axis of polarity. The same thing happens when you spin a bottle of water around and around: the axis down the center induces a vortex that pulls energy in and out (polarity). This back and forth motion from side to side is polarity, and everything in this galaxy, from the tides on our planet to our cranial rhythms to electrons and emotions, moves in this polarity in the same way that anything in the water bottle would move around as you spin it.

Everything in the galaxy experiences this relativity of going back and forth in polarity. Beyond this is the neutral state of the universe, which the yogis and mystics refer to as the universal state of quantum energy and consciousness. In this state there is no polarity, because it is beyond the state of the back and forth of the galaxy. Instead, there is a vast ocean of neutral energy or space.

We have the choice as to where we want to live and have our relativity. Each of us has the choice. By dissolving into the stillpoint state, the body taps into the universal state—and the glands and subtle anatomy activate the sacred nectar to induce unity consciousness. This is the natural state of the human anatomy for which it was designed, and in which we flower when conditions are ripe for our return to our essence.

> *When our planet comes to a perfect point in 2012, we will experience neutrality. This is stillpoint.*

In the same way that flowers are designed to open up and express their essence and fragrance to the light of our star, so too does the human body open up and flower into consciousness as it expresses its essence through the glands and subtle anatomy.

Remember, the universe is a vast ocean of consciousness. We happen to live on a very small, particle-like planet floating through this ocean. In the recent age, most of the folks here have identified with the polarity of our planet. When we shift from body to field, we naturally attune to the neutral state of energy, like the yogis and mystics, and we open up to amazing new possibilities.

DNA and the subtle body weave of energy are examples of scalar waves, which perfectly reflect one another as they activate and open new vistas of possibility. The Scalar Wave Laser and the Stillpoint

Seminar help people dissolve polarity and enter into this new quantum relativity and season. Stillpoint is simply the dissolution of all polarity into the neutral unified field. The process occurs naturally whenever two waves dissolve in perfect symmetry and shift into the quantum state. 2012 is our planet and our star system's symmetrical phase shift-moment. It is a moment in which everything and everyone on the planet has the unique opportunity to dissolve all cell memory, polarity (or karma) and the right- and left-brain linear process, and wake up and return to the universal source from which we all come. In the previous age, everything was based on the linear chronology of the past-present-future progression.

The new season is not based on linear progressions. It is based, rather, in the truth that the past, present and future are all really one moment. During this last season, many people contracted their experience around the body or personality as the reference point for who they were in the universe. This is living in polarity (karma). We prefer the term "polarity," because "karma" implies some obscure thing that is difficult to deal with. In reality, we are simply dealing with basic physics. To clear and dissolve, simply drop into stillpoint and rest in neutrality, much like you would flip the polarity of an old cassette tape or press the delete button on your computer.

In the new season, people are naturally dissolving these contractions and entering the neutrality of the universe, because that is also what is happening to our planet as our star and galaxy form a giant scalar wave, dissolving us all back into universal consciousness. This is stillpoint. As we also drop into this quantum neutral state of energy, we activate quantum wellness, abundance, manifestation, consciousness and the expression of who we really are. When you make the shift and start living in the quantum energy field, you naturally start to activate amazing quantum biological processes, connecting you to the universe and what is, ultimately, beyond the universe.

Stillpoint is not new, or a secret accessible to only a few. All of us are naturally keyed to stillpoint. We have all experienced a moment when suddenly everything was intensified, and all that there was in that moment was real and essential. The reason that folks like to sleep on this planet is that sleep dissolves all of their stress tension, emotions and body rhythms into one wave, one stillpoint, reconnecting them to the universe.

> When you make the shift and start living in the quantum energy field, you naturally start to activate amazing quantum biological processes, connecting you to the universe and what is, ultimately, beyond the universe.

As our planet moves into the new season, opening up to and dissolving into stillpoint deletes polarity and activates the quantum biological process and alchemy that yogis and mystics have been tapping into throughout the ages. In our seminars and in our forthcoming book, *Stillpoint Now*, we share resources that we use to navigate this new quantum season, and how we live from stillpoint. It begins with experiencing stillpoint and using this experience to dissolve polarity, neutralize cellular memory, handle emotions, navigate our lives, manifest abundance and actualize quantum consciousness.

We are on the cusp of a new quantum revolution. Our people are coming back to their senses, literally, as conscious beings of the universe. As our planet and star ripen and shift into this new season, our people are entering the spring flowering of human consciousness. We are all posited to express the essence of who we really are and to embark on a wonderful journey.

Take a deep breath, and as the breath comes out, relax and dissolve into the space between the breath. This is the stillpoint state. There is nothing to do here. Simply dissolve and rest awhile.

Paul and Lillie Weisbart are the developers of Stillpoint Now, a gateway to the new quantum relativity. Rooted in the yogic tradition of living in the "space between the breath," Stillpoint Now is a systematic approach for transition into the new season, enabling people to flower into full expression of this ripening moment for our planet, star, galaxy and universe. Paul and Lillie's unique approach to accessing the quantum neutral unified field state dissolves cellular memory, normalizes body systems, optimizes anti-aging capabilities and activates the glands and higher dimensional subtle body that yogis and mystics have tapped into throughout the ages.

Quantum mystics and inventors of the Scalar Wave Laser, Paul and Lillie lead Stillpoint Now seminars and workshops all over the world, guiding people to clear stress, tension, dis-ease, cellular memory and polarity (karma) in order to help activate the new quantum state of wellness, rejuvenation, manifestation, abundance and consciousness. Their first book, Stillpoint Now, *will be released in 2010. Join them in opening to this wonderful new season and in the flowering of consciousness that is the birthright of all human beings. To learn how you can enter Stillpoint and claim your birthright, visit www.StillpointNow.com.*

Bruce H. Lipton, PhD,
and *Steve Bhaerman*

SPONTANEOUS EVOLUTION AND 2012

We are in a world of crisis. From economic collapse to environmental decay to climate change to war, hunger and poverty, our species seems to be headed fool speed ahead on a fast track to a train wreck. But what if these crises presented the greatest opportunity in recorded history—conscious evolution?

Our book, *Spontaneous Evolution: Our Positive Future and a Way to Get There from Here,* offers both the hope and challenge that we can safely navigate this dark passage to a healthier future. The good news is that biology and evolution are on our side. Contrary to what conventional science and religion have been telling us, evolution is neither random nor predetermined, but rather an intelligent dance between organism and environment. When conditions are ripe—through either crisis or opportunity—something unpredictable happens to bring the biosphere into a new balance, at a higher level of coherence.

While we often perceive examples of *spontaneous remission* as miraculous healings that happen by the grace of God, looking a little deeper we see something else at work. Quite often these fortunate individuals actively participate in their own healing by consciously or unconsciously making a key, significant change in their beliefs and behaviors.

So here is the bad news *and* the good news. The story of human life on Earth is yet to be determined. Spontaneous evolution will depend on whether or not we humans are willing to make changes in our individual and collective beliefs and behaviors, and whether or not we are able to make these changes in time. For millennia, our

> *Like it or not, our future depends on the choices we make as a species.*

spiritual teachers have been pointing us in the direction of relatedness and love. Now, science is confirming that ancient wisdom. We are, each and all, cells in the body of an evolving giant super-organism we call *humanity*. Because humans have free will, we can choose to either rise to that new level of emergence or, in the manner of dinosaurs, fall by the wayside. Like it or not, our future depends on the choices we make as a species.

ALL YOU NEED IS LOVE—REALLY!
From Jesus to The Beatles, the message of love is all around us. And we humans have spent the past two thousand years both hearing and resisting it. Perhaps now that science is echoing ancient wisdom in this regard, we might actually heed the message. Thanks to the current paradigm of scientific materialism, most of us believe (if not consciously, than unconsciously) that life is a dog-eat-dog rat race, a dire competition where only the fittest survive. However, science now tells us that this Darwinian view is distorted. In actuality, environments survive and evolve as systems. Whatever helps to balance a system thrives, while that which doesn't fit doesn't survive. Thus, the real evolutionary principle is survival of the "fittingest."

Our planet is facing what scientists are calling the "Sixth Great Mass Extinction." The previous five were apparently caused by objects from outer space, such as comets or asteroids, hitting the Earth. This time, the cause comes from "inner space"—our own invisible beliefs that have spun us outside the web of life. Beginning with monotheistic religion telling us that we humans are superior and apart from other creatures on the planet, exacerbated by scientific materialism insisting human technology has the power to "conquer" nature, we have focused so heavily on our fitness as individuals, we have failed to recognize that our fitness as a species is up for examination.

However, the most transformational tool in our human toolkit—and the one we've largely ignored for the past two millennia—is love. This love we are talking about is not some mushy-gushy sentiment, but the glue that holds our world together. According to Dr. Leonard Laskow, a surgeon who discovered his own innate ability to heal with love and wrote about it in *Healing With Love: A Breakthrough Mind/Body Medical Program for Healing Yourself and Others,* "Love is a universal pattern of resonant energy." In this sense, two or more tuning forks vibrating together are in love with each other, just as two or more humans can resonate in a palpable field of connectedness, joy, even ecstasy. Love, he said, "is the universal harmonic."

LOVE AND EVOLUTION

If indeed love is a resonant harmonic, then a case can be made for evolution being the evolution of love itself. From the first spark of life, ignited by waves of light impregnating particles of matter on Earth, every stage of evolution has involved two things: greater connection and greater awareness. While we should beware of anthropomorphizing cells—they *hate it* when we do that—in a very important sense, when single cells joined to become multi-cell organisms, they "surrendered" to a higher level of organization, and "agreed" to live in harmony. In other words, love.

The same has been true of individuals affiliating in tribes, and tribes affiliating as nations. At each stage, individuals (or groups of individuals) have become *aware* of how *connecting* in community would enhance their wellbeing. Taking a cue from the Iroquois Nation, America's founders designed a system in which individual states gave up their right to arm themselves against one another. Think for a moment what it would have meant if states had had armed borders, and the inevitability of border skirmishes. America's prosperity has been due, in part, to not having to spend resources defending against other Americans.

On a worldwide scale, imagine what we could do with the trillions of dollars we spend on weaponry. Certainly, an argument can be made that while the vast majority of us may be peace-loving, we would still have to defend ourselves against those who aren't. This is true. However, we are all too commonly mobilized by our "leaders" against a perceived enemy, when in actuality the true "enemy" is the field of beliefs that reinforce an absence of love—and the misleaders who manipulate that field.

A WORLD IN CRISIS = A WORLD OF OPPORTUNITIES

Meanwhile, in the collective consciousness there has been a growing awareness that, to quote Dorothy, "We're not in Kansas anymore." Whether it's the evangelicals speaking about the Rapture, scientists warning of the Sixth Great Extinction, or those who see "2012" as some transformational watershed date, there is an understanding that we are on the threshold of profound change. Meanwhile, old structures and ways of being seem to be crumbling all around us. Our institutions—from hospitals to schools to banks to our own government—are failing, and seem to be unfixable. What's going on?

> *From within the dying population, a new breed of cells begins to emerge, called imaginal cells.*

To better understand the opportunity hidden in the crisis, consider the tale of another world in transition. Imagine you are a single cell among millions that comprise a growing caterpillar. The structure around you has been operating like a well-oiled machine, and the larva world has been creeping along predictably. Then one day, the machine begins to shudder and shake. The system begins to fail. Cells begin to commit suicide. There is a sense of darkness and impending doom.

From within the dying population, a new breed of cells begins to emerge, called imaginal cells. Clustering in community, they devise a plan to create something entirely new from the wreckage. Out of the decay arises a great flying machine—a butterfly—that enables the survivor cells to escape from the ashes and experience a beautiful world, far beyond imagination. Here is the amazing thing: the caterpillar and the butterfly have the exact same DNA. They are the same organism, but are receiving and responding to different organizing signals.

That is where we are today. When we read the newspaper and watch the evening news, we see the media reporting a decaying caterpillar world. And yet, everywhere, human imaginal cells are awakening to a new possibility. They are clustering, communicating and tuning into a new, coherent signal of love. We are now between "two worlds"—the caterpillar world where our future is limited by our creepy-crawly past, and the butterfly world where humanity can soar to reach its highest potential. Unlike the shift from caterpillar to butterfly, however, transformation of humanity is not inevitable. It requires our participation. We have the choice to live in and reinforce the limitations imposed by fear and past programming. Or, we can attune ourselves to the new signal of love, and live that instead.

Consequently, what we collectively imagine to be true about 2012 is what is most likely to manifest. It all depends on the pictures we put into our heads. On one hand, we have the *2012* movie, that offers up a heaping helping of mass destruction as inevitable and even links to a fictional Institute for Human Continuity, where filmgoers can enter a lottery to be part of a chosen few to be rescued from global holocaust. Meanwhile, another film, *Shift of the Ages*, offers the wisdom of Mayan elders. They tell us that indeed we *are* on the cusp of transformational change—but only if our species changes our mission from survival of the fittest to thrival of the fittingest. In other words, spontaneous remission depends on "spontaneous remissioning."

2012 AND THE "END OF TIME"

One of the more fearsome notions about the 2012 prophecies is that it will be the "end of time." If we remain stuck in the idea of time as an absolute, this prospect would indicate that the end of time is the end of life. However, as quantum physics is coming to understand, everything that has ever been or will be exists in an eternal Now, and through our perceptions—including time—we sort events into past, present and future. In our book, we even cite experiments that show that we are not only able to influence future events, we can influence past events as well!

> In other words, spontaneous remission depends on "spontaneous remissioning."

For the purposes of this writing, however, there is a simpler and more encouraging interpretation of "the end of time" that suggests a pathway to our fullest potential: the end of living in our old stories, those that keep us repeating the same patterns over and over again. Perhaps these "end times" indicate that we as a species heal and resolve our old stories... so we are free to write and live into a new one. When we recognize that so much of who we imagine we are is based on programmed, "invisible" beliefs, we can begin to see that this programming is the one thing we have in common. The entire notion of "blame" at that point seems absurd. As the Biblical injunction says, "Forgive them because they know not what they do."

In this forgiveness and liberation from blame, we can accept responsibility. That is, we can choose to respond differently. In healing these stories of separation, we can embrace the new story that we are each and all cells in a new organism. A miraculous healing awaits this planet once we accept our new responsibility to collectively tend the Garden rather than fight over the turf. When a critical mass of people truly own this belief in their hearts and minds and actually begin living from this truth, our world will emerge from the darkness in what will amount to a *spontaneous evolution*.

Bruce H. Lipton, PhD, is an internationally recognized leader in bridging science and spirit. Early in his career as a cellular biologist, Dr. Lipton's discoveries presaged one of today's most important fields of study, the science of epigenetics. His scientific approach deepened his understanding of cell biology, highlighting the mechanisms by which the mind controls bodily functions, and implied the existence of an immortal spirit. Dr. Lipton has since taken his award-winning medical school lectures to the public, lecturing about leading-edge science and how it dovetails with mind-body medicine and spiritual principles. A sought-after keynote speaker, he has been featured on hundreds of television and radio shows. Dr. Lipton is the author of The Biology of Belief *(2008) and co-author of* Spontaneous Evolution: Our Positive Future and a Way to Get There From Here *(2009). To learn more about Dr. Lipton, visit www.BruceLipton.com.*

Steve Bhaerman is an internationally known author, humorist and workshop leader. For the past twenty-two years he has written and performed as Swami Beyondananda, the "Cosmic Comic." In 1980, Steve co-founded Pathways *magazine in Ann Arbor, Michigan, one of the first publications bringing together holistic health, personal growth, spirituality and politics. As the Swami, Steve is the author of* Driving Your Own Karma *(1989),* When You See a Sacred Cow, Milk It For All It's Worth *(1993),* Duck Soup for the Soul *(1999) and* Swami for Precedent: A 7-Step Plan to Heal the Body Politic and Cure Electile Dysfunction *(2004). He is the co-author of* Spontaneous Evolution: Our Positive Future and a Way to Get There From Here *(2009). To learn more about Steve and Swami, visit www.WakeUpLaughing.com.*

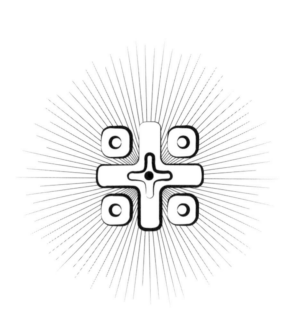

Carl Johan Calleman, PhD

THE RIGHT END DATE

For some time now, many American New Age gurus talking about "2012" have been repeating a scenario that they claim is based on the Mayan calendar, and goes essentially like this: The Mayan calendar is based on the twenty-six-thousand-year long precessional cycle and leads to a "galactic alignment" on December 21, 2012, when change is suddenly (and inexplicably) going to come down from the sky.

Since most of these "experts" have never researched the Mayan calendar, they do not know—or chose to ignore—some very basic facts: First, that among the thousands of inscriptions the ancient Maya left behind, a 26,000-year cycle is never mentioned. Second, not a single Mayan text mentions a "galactic alignment" at the end of the 5,125-year Long Count that we are approaching. Third, the Maya are known to have changed calendrical dates for political reasons, similar to how the Christian church celebrates the birth of Christ on December 25, even though this is now known not to be the right date.

Because of this suppression of facts, it is not surprising that the community of Mayanist scholars has consistently rejected the New Age view of the end date, which also ignores the message in the few remaining descriptions that the ancient Maya left behind. Nonetheless, the combination of this precessional theory with mainstream projections of an end of the world—such as the History Channel's documentary *Doomsday 2012* or the film *2012*—serves to block people from understanding what exactly the Mayan calendar tells us about the future of our planet.

The New Age gurus leading people to believe in the December 21, 2012, date have thus assumed a large responsibility that they do not necessarily have the knowledge to back up. Mostly, they are not even pondering the possibility that their violations of the principles upon which the Mayan calendar was based may come to have disastrous consequences for the possibilities of their followers to prepare for and consciously participate in the birth of a new world. In my view, it is thus important to have a solid scientific understanding of the Mayan calendar if the promise of a millennium of peace is to be delivered.

> *In my view, it is thus important to have a solid scientific understanding of the Mayan calendar if the promise of a millennium of peace is to be delivered.*

Only one Mayan inscription of the end date from ancient times remains, at the Tortuguero monument. It says that, on this date, "nine gods will descend." Although the inscription only surfaced in the public discussion recently, it verifies the model I presented in my first book (published in 1994 in Swedish). To understand what the descent of nine gods may mean, it is important to realize that the Mayan concept of god is not as personalized as in European cultures, where gods were seen as individuals. Among the Maya, gods were often seen as cosmic forces associated with certain time periods.

According to this model, nine different levels of cosmic evolution, each developing according to an increased frequency and creating a speed-up of time, will simultaneously come to an end at this end date (meaning that nine cosmic forces will manifest, or nine "gods" will descend). This view of nine wave movements coming to their completion is supported by massive evidence, and it is the only theory about the meaning of the Mayan calendar that has received any recognition in the established scientific community. The importance of the nine levels of the cosmos is also evidenced by the many Mayan pyramids, which are built in nine stories in central locations of their temple sites.

> *A hallmark of a serious scientific theory is, instead, that it gives rise to testable predictions. This is indeed the case for the October 28, 2011, end date.*

The contemporary spokesman of the Mayan council of elders, Don Alejandro Oxlaj, regards the December 21, 2012, date as a miscalculation by archaeologists, and emphasizes the prophecy of the return of 13 Ahau, which is the last energy of the Sacred Mayan Calendar. In line with this, I have advocated that the true date when all nine cosmic forces are coming to their fulfillment must be a day with the energy of 13 Ahau, namely October 28, 2011. This has very significant consequences for how we may understand the Mayan calendar, and is a logically understandable process leading to the birth of a new world.

Since two different end dates—December 21, 2012, and October 28, 2011—have been suggested, we may then wonder how to know which is right. In science, this is done by determining which hypothesis generates verifiable predictions. Unfortunately, advocates of a galactic alignment on December 21, 2012, never make any predictions, meaning that their end date, like all beliefs, is not testable.

A hallmark of a serious scientific theory is, instead, that it gives rise to testable predictions.

This is indeed the case for the October 28, 2011, end date. For instance, in my book *The Mayan Calendar and the Transformation of Consciousness*, I predicted the economic collapse in November 2007 based on the Mayan calendar. Economists now agree that the downturn began in December of 2007—meaning that, based on the October 28, 2011, end date, the wave movement of our present economy can be understood from the Mayan calendar.

This prediction was actually formulated already in my first book in English, *Solving the Greatest Mystery of Our Time: The Mayan Calendar* (written in 1999; published in 2001), and was a direct parallel to Edgar Cayce's famous prediction of the time that the New York Stock Exchange would crash. However, my prediction was made about ten years in advance, and thus much earlier than any professional economist even considered such an economic meltdown. That these predictions were made in advance can be verified by anyone, showing the predictive power of understanding the shifting energies of the Mayan calendar. Those advocating the December 21, 2012, date failed to predict the economic decline, and they cannot credit themselves with having made even one accurate prediction based on the Mayan calendar. This means that their end date lacks a foundation in reality and so very likely will lead people astray, since in real life we need to know something about when things will happen.

As mentioned, the Mayan calendar describes nine evolutionary wave movements, and this wave nature is behind the fact that history is rarely linear and more often proceeds via quantum jumps. Hence, the Mayan calendar does not describe the usual continuous time that our clocks do. Mayan time is instead a quantum phenomenon, and its various shift points were, in ancient times, believed to emanate from the World Tree or the Tree of Life, which also goes by the name of the Heart of the Heavens.

As I describe in my book, *The Purposeful Universe*, modern physics has recently discovered that there indeed is a center to the whole universe (in which our galaxy is like a mere speck of dust), meaning that its entire evolution may emanate from an intelligent center, which is also what we know that the Maya believed.

What is important here is that an understanding of Mayan time as quantized provides a meaningful way of looking at the so-called end date: a way in which it is not even potentially a preset end of the world. In a quantum model, *the end date simply reflects the point in time when the Cosmic Tree of Life attains its highest quantum state and this is reflected in life on Earth.* It is only on this basis that it is rationally understandable for this state to lead to the birth of a new world and a millennium of peace in the "New Jerusalem" (as it is called in the *Book of Revelation*). To use a Hindu metaphor, the attainment of this highest state means liberation from the wheels (cycles) of karma.

> *This means that their end date lacks a foundation in reality and so very likely will lead people astray, since in real life we need to know something about when things will happen.*

As the student of the Mayan calendar will know, almost all conflicts and warfare in the history of mankind actually originate in quantum shifts in cosmic energies—and only as those come to an end is there any serious reason to hope for the emergence of a world in harmony.

The figure below shows how the actual wave movements of the Mayan calendar—the two highest levels of evolution of the cosmos, the eighth and the ninth, the Galactic and the Universal Underworlds—are playing out. The economic meltdown that began with NIGHT 5 is, in this perspective, not merely a "depression." It is, instead, the beginning of the end of the cycles of the economy. Yet, since we know from the study of the Mayan calendar that the NIGHTS are the time periods in which the economy shrank, we can

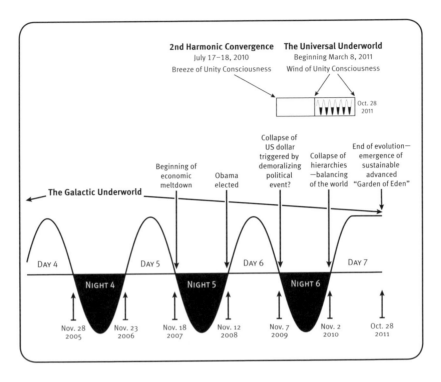

make some predictions as to what will happen in the end of these economic cycles.

I think there is every reason to expect great hardships in the world later in the sixth NIGHT, possibly leading to global revolutionary change. An intensified economic meltdown may also be seen as a protective mechanism for the planet, as it halts the incessant economic growth that has led it to the brink of ecological disaster. The first thing a cancer doctor needs to do before any recovery can take place is to stop the cancer's growth—and, in the cosmic plan, the planet is not meant to die. The "New Jerusalem" is not a stressful growth economy that threatens the survival of the global ecosystem.

Knowing the exact end date of the Mayan calendar is a critical issue, since it directly determines how we relate to the future. To have the end date right is the only chance people have to know what cosmic energy they are experiencing in the present moment; the effect of this energy on life and the economy; and when the quantum shifts between these energies will occur.

Such a view, where evolution is driven by cosmic energies, may however be offensive to many human egos, since it means that we are not creating our own reality. Instead, this is emanating from the divine source, which may be the reason that many deny the true Mayan calendar. After October 28, 2011, however, it will be meaningful to talk about humanity, or sections thereof, creating its reality.

Carl Johan Calleman has a PhD in Physical Biology from the University of Stockholm. With his Solving the Greatest Mystery of Our Time: The Mayan Calendar *(Garev, 2001) he initiated the evidence-based study of the Mayan calendar, which was followed by* The Mayan Calendar and the Transformation of Consciousness *(Bear and Co., 2004) and* The Purposeful Universe *(Bear and Co., 2009). To learn more about Carl, visit www.Calleman.com. (See also www.Maya-Portal.net.)*

THE HOPI/TIBETAN PROPHECIES

Something wonderful is happening. We are entering the "Time of Never Ending Peace," what the Tibetans call "Shambala" and the Hopi refer to as "The Fifth World." We just have to hang on a little longer to see it all unfold. This is the promise of the "Hopi/Tibetan Prophecy."

A Cherokee by ethnicity, I was adopted into the Hopi Tribe. Grandfather Martin Gashweseoma, the "Keeper of the Sacred Tablets of the Fire Clan," asked me to represent the Hopi side of the Prophecy. Ven. Bhakha Tulku Rinpoche asked me to share the Tibetan side of the Prophecy. He is the reincarnation of Vairotsana, a disciple of the Buddha Padmasambhava, who spoke of the Tibetan Prophecy. I have been asked to be the "Messenger of the Hopi/Tibetan Prophecy." I am not the Messenger of the Hopi Prophecy, nor the Messenger of the Tibetan Prophecy. I have been asked to share the Prophecy that connects the Hopi and the Tibetans. This is not my Prophecy. I am merely honoring a request to share it with the world.

It all began in 2001, when Tibetan lama monks came to my house looking for my son, who was four years old at the time. It was then that I first learned that since the Tibetans lost their country in 1959, the reincarnated lamas (Tibetan priests) and *tulkus* (enlightened Tibetan lamas) were being born in the West. During that year many Tibetans came to see my son, and many have visited since.

In December of 2001, I was asked to take my son to see Ven. Bhakha Tulku Rinpoche, who confirmed that my son was actually a reincarnated Tibetan lama. He gave us a rock with ancient writing on it. In January of 2002, a woman came to my house and shared the Hopi Prophecy about a sacred rock with a missing piece, and explained that the Hopi were still waiting for that piece. She asked if the Tibetans had given my son a rock with ancient writing on it, and when I showed it to her, she asked me to come to the Hopi reservation and bring the rock with us. This is how I first met Grandfather Martin Gashweseoma—*in this life.*

> *I have been asked to share the prophecy that connects the Hopi and the Tibetans. This is not my Prophecy. I am merely honoring a request to share it with the world.*

When I met Grandfather, I realized I remembered him from dreams I'd had since I was a little girl. Since I was a child, I have had dreams and visions about what would happen in this time we are living in now. In meeting Grandfather Martin Gashweseoma, my dream life and my waking life came together, and since then I've traveled to Hopi to study the Hopi Prophecy and the story of the Hopi Prophecy Rock. When I am home, far away from the Hopi, Grandfather communicates with me through my dreams, sending me messages to share with the world.

I have spent many years studying with the Tibetans, and have taken Bodhisattva Vows with His Holiness the 14th Dalai Lama. This means I have made a promise to attempt to attain enlightenment with the intention of remaining in the cycle of *samsara* (rebirth) until all sentient beings are liberated from suffering. I have also been initiated and trained by Hopi Elders, and taken many empowerments with the Tibetans, all in preparation for serving as the "Messenger of the Hopi/Tibetan Prophecy."

I would like to share with you what I was taught about the connection between the Hopi and Tibetan Prophecies. There is a Hopi Prophecy that begins:

"When the Iron Eagle flies
and the Horses have wheels
Our long lost Brother will return
from the East…"

The Hopi Prophecy continues and takes at least eight days to tell in its entirety. Part of the Hopi Prophecy describes a time when their "brother with the red hat and red capes will return from the sky" with information that will help the Hopi during the difficult "Time of Purification." There is a matching Tibetan Prophecy, shared by Padmasambhava, stating:

"When the Iron Eagle flies the sky
and stone bridges cover rivers.
Horses with wheels will run on roads.
East will meet West.
Red People will meet Red People.
At that time my teachings will benefit the world."

In 1974 His Holiness the Gyalwa Karmapa, the 16th Karmapa (head of the Karma Kagyu school of Buddhism), was the first Tibetan to arrive in Hopi. His visit activated the Realization of the "Hopi/Tibetan Prophecies." Since then there have been many meetings between the Hopi and the Tibetans over the years.

The message of the Hopi Prophecy is illustrated on the Hopi Prophecy Rock on the Hopi Reservation. The Hopi Prophecy Rock foretells World War I and World War II, and then illustrates two paths from which the world would choose. The "Path of the Two-Hearted" leads to a nuclear World War III and annihilation of life as we know it. The "Path of the One-Hearted" leads to "The Fifth World." If humans choose to remain noble and live the instructions of Maussau, the Creator, we will walk the "Path of the One-Hearted," avoid nuclear World War III and enter the "Time of Never Ending Peace."

I have been told to share with you that, in the last few years, we have passed over into "The Fifth World."

Up until very recently, many of the Hopi Elders were not certain that we would choose the "Path of the One-Hearted." Fortunately, I have been told that in the last few years, we have turned a corner. Many Holy and Noble people have performed the sacred rituals and ceremonies, asking Mother Earth to give us another chance. An evolution of consciousness has occurred just in time to save our planet.

I have been told to share with you that, in the last few years, we have passed over into "The Fifth World." With 2012 approaching, there are so many doomsday stories circulating, describing an impending time of catastrophe and destruction. This is why I was asked to tell the story of the "Two Paths of the Hopi Prophecy Rock," to tell you that *the day after* December 21, 2012 is actually going to herald a time of great peace.

The "Hopi/Tibetan Prophecies" talk about "The Shift," explaining that it is a literal shift that has to do with the Axis of the North and South poles of the Earth. The Hopi Creation story speaks of the "Axis Twins" who will return in human form during the "Time of Purification" to help *keep the balance*. I have been told that Grandfather Martin Gashweseoma and Ven. Bhaka Tulku Rinpoche are the "Axis Twins," and because these two Holy Men of One Heart have lived and dedicated their lives to their responsibilities along with other Holy people, we will make it through "The Shift" if we complete it in 2012.

People have asked me if I believe that the rock Ven. Bhaka Tulku Rinpoche gave us to take to Grandfather Martin Gashweseoma was the actual missing part of the "Sacred Tablets of the Fire Clan." I do not think it is the actual rock; I think it is symbolic. I do believe that the *message* on the rock is indeed the message that the Hopi were waiting for. The message on the rock is "*OM MANI PADME HUM*," a Tibetan mantra which loosely translates as "Compassion." I believe that the message of compassion and loving kindness that the Tibetans have brought to the West is part of what tipped the balance, helping us save our world and choose the "Path of the One-Hearted."

> *I believe that the message of compassion and loving kindness that the Tibetans have brought to the West is part of what tipped the balance, helping us save our world and choose the "Path of the One-Hearted."*

Paradoxically, the Tibetans being driven out of their country, as Padmasambhava predicted, created the causes and conditions for the Message of Compassion to be heard all over the world.

There is a Hopi saying: "We are the ones we have been waiting for." *We* turned the corner; *we* saved our world, *we* chose the right path, the path of Never-Ending Peace. So as chaotic as the world may appear right now, it is an illusion. Something wonderful *is* happening.

Kymberlee Ruff is a licensed psychotherapist in private practice. In her thirty years working in the field of psychology, Kymberlee studied with many brilliant minds, including Dr. Marshall Rosenberg, the founder of the Center for Non-Violent Communication. She has studied the spectrum of psychology, from traditional Jungian analysis with clinical psychologists to "The Dreamtime" with an Aboriginal shaman. Today, she integrates the old ways of the First People into her psychotherapy practice.

In 2002, Kymberlee was called to become the "Messenger of the Hopi/Tibetan Prophecies" by an unusual sequence of events. Since that time she has committed to sharing the message of peace and compassion the two cultures share. Kymberlee assisted the History Channel and other production companies in the making of documentaries about the Hopi, helped with pilgrimages to Hopi and with fundraisers for both the Hopi and Tibetan people. Kymberlee took the "Vows of the Bodhisattva" with His Holiness the Dalai Lama. She was asked to become a Native Elder on July 14, 2006.

Born in the Cherokee Nation in Arkansas, Kymberlee is one quarter Cherokee by ethnicity. She lives in Santa Barbara where she is raising her two wonderful sons. To learn more about Kymberlee, visit www.KymberleeRuff.com.

Kymberlee Ruff contributed this piece without compensation. She does not receive any money for her involvement with the Hopi and the Tibetans, as long ago she made a Covenant with Maussau never to sell the Prophecies. May All Beings Benefit.

Daniel Pinchbeck

AFTER THE DISASTER

Recently, a two-hundred-fifty-million dollar film linked 2012 with a mass wipeout of humanity from earth crust displacement and super-volcano spew. The spectacle seemed designed to curtail any deeper thought or discussion of the subject by making it appear ridiculous. Apparently, I was parodied in the film, as *The New York Times* noted: "Though not much is made of the Mayan angle, the most amusing character, a doomsday prophet and radio broadcaster played by Woody Harrelson, seems in hair, beard and interests to have been drawn along the predictive lines of the real author Daniel Pinchbeck *(2012: The Return of Quetzalcoatl)*."

Although my ideas run counter to what the filmmakers propose, I allowed myself to be incorporated into their marketing and promotion machine. I was one of three "2012 experts" flown to Jackson Hole, Wyoming, to address the global press, and then to Los Angeles for the appropriately black-carpeted premiere. I accepted the invitations because I hoped to use the opportunity to convey a different message. As the media reduced my ideas to sound bites or hopelessly distorted them, I felt as if a mask of cultural fears and misconceptions was being projected onto my face. This was not surprising, but it was still deeply unsettling. I don't pretend to be a "2012 expert" or a "doomsday prophet." I am not a specialist or scholar, but a generalist, journalist and freelance philosopher. In my last book I described, as truthfully as I could, my exploration of subjects including psychedelic shamanism and indigenous prophecy.

While a number of visionaries propose that something radical, absolutely astonishing and unprecedented is going to happen as we pass through the 2012 portal—galactic synchronization, mass DMT activation, sudden ascension, a huge solar storm, a galactic superwave—I have never pretended to have an answer.

I don't know what the Classic Maya understood about our time through their visionary experiences, or what means they used to establish that the end of their Long Count calendar would be the hinge of a shift between "World Ages." Even if John Major Jenkins's theory that they correlated this shift with the astronomical alignment of the winter solstice sun rising at the dark rift in the center of the Milky Way is correct, we don't know why this particular alignment would have a tangible effect on our world. While a cycle of over five thousand years ends in 2012, there is little evidence the Maya expected any particular event to occur at that precise juncture. At the same time, some contemporary astrophysicists are now concerned that a sudden increase in solar activity could shut down the electrical grid sometime in 2012, while some economists foresee a global financial meltdown coming as we approach the end date.

Despite all of the question marks around the subject, "2012" can be useful as a focusing lens and an opportunity to rethink the direction of our current civilization. Instead of fixating on any future event, we need to realize that any positive transformation, whether in 2012 or after, will only be the result of deliberate actions and conscious choices made by human beings in the present.

Despite the intensifying evolutionary pressures we face and the telescoped timeframe in which progress and change now occurs, we remain a half-awake, half-conscious species. As individuals, we tend to be vain, fragile, self-serving, ego-centered. The organizations and institutions we create reflect our individual flaws. This much is inarguable: We find ourselves in a window of opportunity where we either radically change our direction as a species, or face devastating consequences.

We are at that threshold where, as the social ecologist Murray Bookchin put it, our world "will either undergo revolutionary changes, so far-reaching in character that humanity will totally transform its social relations and its very conception of life, or it will suffer an apocalypse that may well end humanity's tenure on the planet." Examining trends in climate change and species extinction, the esteemed scientist James Lovelock, who developed the Gaia hypothesis, now thinks there could be 150 million people left alive at the end of this century. Other scientists share his ominous outlook. As resources such as fuel and fresh water become scarce, it is quite likely we will see even more horrific wars, masses of refugees, famines, droughts, pandemics and revolutions.

> This much is inarguable: We find ourselves in a window of opportunity where we either radically change our direction as a species, or face devastating consequences.

If the outlook from a purely empirical perspective looks bleak, the good news is that science has ignored some crucial factors. One is the possibility that human beings, through an evolution of consciousness, could develop a regenerative culture that contributes to the health of the biosphere. In the 1960s, the design scientist Buckminster Fuller proposed that society could be redesigned to be "comprehensively successful" for everyone on Earth.

In the short term, we could become far more flexible and resilient, instituting a global program that re-localizes basic essentials such as growing food, producing energy and making clothes and shelter, while liberating knowledge as a free resource and commonwealth. We could institute "cradle to cradle" manufacturing practices, and use satyagraha techniques to stop the spread of GMOs. We could replace money, as a basic instrument, by new systems for exchanging value that support collaboration and trust over competition and self-interest. Despite the system's inertia, we have the capacity to restore the natural systems we have corrupted, and create a new planetary culture based on communality of interest.

Another factor ignored by science and the mainstream is the reality of paranormal phenomena, psychic energy, or what Carl Jung called "the reality of the Psyche." There is much evidence for the existence of all sorts of extraordinary psychic effects, and many people have direct experience of such phenomena.

As an analogy, we can consider the recent discovery and application of electricity. Once engineers learned how to conduct and store electricity in the nineteenth century, we transformed the entire Earth in a blink of evolutionary time. If we discovered reliable means to access, use and channel psychic energy, we might participate in an extremely rapid evolution of consciousness and society. José Argüelles has proposed that this future culture of ours would be "psycho-technic;" applying our modern technical capacities to the realms of the psyche that modern society lost contact with in the last centuries.

> Despite the system's inertia, we have the capacity to restore the natural systems we have corrupted, and create a new planetary culture based on communality of interest.

The possibility for a rapid regeneration of human culture is predicated on a great awakening happening quickly—before ecological meltdown leads to systemic breakdown. People need to awaken spiritually, to realize the many dimensions of psychic life beyond those accepted by modern culture—and, at the same time, bring those realizations down into their daily lives and make deep changes in our society.

Spiritual realization needs to be integrated with social commitment and direct action. Since the biosphere is now directly threatened by our post-industrial civilization, retreat from society is no longer possible or desirable. No matter whether we like it or not, each of is, inevitably, a social and political agent whose smallest actions have a direct influence on other people and the world around us. Our current culture enshrines irresponsibility, greed and waste. If the human species wants to survive, the civilization that replaces this one is going to have a different set of values and a revamped operating system.

> *If the human species wants to survive,*
> *the civilization that replaces this one is*
> *going to have a different set of values*
> *and a revamped operating system.*

While it is conceivable that 2012 may see some sudden quantum shift in human consciousness or an alien landing on the White House lawn, it is also possible that we have a much longer struggle ahead of us. In that case, the end of the Long Count may still be significant as the hinge of a transition in our species' awareness. An ever-growing segment of humanity is becoming conscious of the culture of domination that has degraded the biosphere, annihilated local cultures, and locked us in a prison of constricted awareness. As more and more of us realize this, we will unify our intention to undertake the difficult work of superseding it.

Daniel Pinchbeck is the author of 2012: The Return of Quetzalcoatl *and* Breaking Open the Head: A Psychedelic Journey into the Heart of Contemporary Shamanism. *His articles have appeared in* The New York Times *magazine,* Esquire, Wired, The Village Voice, LA

Weekly, ArtForum, Arthur *and many other publications. Daniel is currently the editorial director of the web magazine* Reality Sandwich *(www.RealitySandwich.com). He is the co-founder of the social network Evolver (www.Evolver.net), which supports the Evolver Social Movement, bringing together local communities that share an interest in conscious evolution and in developing alternatives to mainstream culture. Daniel is also the executive producer of the "PostModern Times" series of interviews, directed by João Amorim, and is featured in Amorim's upcoming documentary,* 2012: Time for Change *(www.2012TimeForChange.com). Daniel's book,* Notes from the End Times, *is expected in October of 2010.*

Marilyn Mandala Schlitz, PhD

LIVING BETWEEN STORIES

The year 2012, for me, is not so much about a moment in time as it is about collaborating and participating in a shifting world-view. This truly remarkable period in human history is unprecedented in its complexity. We are witnessing an incredible acceleration in the pace of our increasingly connected lives and systems, which leads to a sense of uncertainty. However, it also offers us an opportunity to connect, to grow and to bridge our differences in a multiplicity of new ways. It feels, in some fundamental way, as though we are living between stories.

The old models are being calibrated and, in some ways, celebrated. We see enormous achievements in the physical world using materialist science, such as an orbiting space station, studies of the human genome, and all the potentials that are coming from the neurosciences and molecular biology. The Internet, which is contributing greatly to the exponential accelerations being felt in this period of time, is also playing a significant role in linking us together and giving us a sense of shared identity. For the first time, all the world's wisdom, spiritual and religious traditions are readily accessible. There's a way, now, in which this kind of globalization is part of a paradigm shift.

So while 2012 holds much richness in terms of people's individual navigation systems, I believe it is also a symbolic moment of reflection on this between-ness, this interim stage in which we are moving from modernity and a sense of control toward something that is evolving more quickly than our imaginations can keep up with. It becomes a marker for the imaginal, a point at which to anchor and poise ourselves before moving into what is next and really *living into* this new decade of the twenty-first century.

> *It feels, in some fundamental way, as though we are living between stories.*

We are not simply moving from one paradigm to another—rather, I believe we are moving through a moment where resilience is required to deal with the sheer multiplicity of worldviews. So if there is a shift in paradigm, it is one that is forcing us to confront a lot of different perspectives. Bridging different stories and different ways of knowing offers potentials for great breakthrough, both for ourselves and for future generations.

We are in a process of continuous change, and there are many traditions that can help us to reflect on these changes. Change is nothing new; neither is our desire for continuity. People get into comfort zones. Our brains become comfortable and our cultures become comfortable with certain ways of operating. But in order for transformation to occur on a level that is beyond a steady, comfortable state, some shaking up of what has become habitual is needed. That is certainly happening today. We are meeting in places of profound difference, places where different worldviews, different assumptions and different trajectories on the path forward are coming into contact.

So what happens when differences come into contact? We know that conflict and confrontation occur when people hold intolerance and an inability to reconcile conflicting points of view. Another possible outcome is co-option, where one dominant truth system overpowers another. We see this in the widespread reach of Western materialism. Doing field research in the Ecuadorian Amazon, for example, I've seen someone who lives deep in the forest wearing a Chicago Bulls t-shirt. This convergence of story happens gradually; people in the Amazon see that people from the north have things they do not, so they change their vision of what they want. Thus, gradually, their internal worldview and belief system change, too. The third possible outcome of this meeting of difference is creativity, and that potential breakthrough comes from our ability to hold paradox. The Dalai Lama, for instance, who represents a faith and philosophical tradition, is also deeply interested in neuroscience and quantum physics. Here we have two different systems, two different stories *engaging* each other—but that doesn't mean that they are going to *become* each other.

> We are meeting in places of profound difference, places where different worldviews, different assumptions and different trajectories on the path forward are coming into contact.

As a noetic scientist, I especially love the idea that science, a truth system with particular sets of assumptions and methods, can engage with our inner world in a way that reveals more about the human condition and can help promote our well-being on every level. It is a time for the inner and outer worlds to meet, and a lot of new tools are being offered to help establish this engagement. This is hugely significant because, historically, science has completely ignored consciousness and inner experience.

If we can learn to ride this wave of creativity, celebrating pluralism and all that our confluences of difference have to offer, then we will develop cognitively for what comes next, building up our resilience for managing change, rather than succumbing to fundamentalism or co-option. Like fish in water, we don't really notice the environment that surrounds us, but it's making a lot of demands on our attention.

We used to just write letters; now we have voicemail, email, Facebook, Twitter. So attention is a fundamental issue for the twenty-first century. How can we learn to nourish our capacities to attend to both what is important for our well-being *and* the choices we make when meeting in places of difference, especially with all these distractions around us?

> *If we can learn to ride this wave of creativity, celebrating pluralism and all that our confluences of difference have to offer, then we will develop cognitively for what comes next, building up our resilience for managing change, rather than succumbing to fundamentalism or co-option.*

Focus on intention is a really big piece of how we direct ourselves. What intention do we bring as individuals and collective participants in these various worldviews? It's also incredibly important, in this time of great acceleration, change and a global communications network, for us social animals to have a strong sense of conviviality and a place to ground us. And yet we're living in a culture that is increasingly alienating to that impulse. Holding paradox is a kind of agility that can be cultivated through intentional grounding in community and nourished through transformational practices such as meditation.

So one of the shifts into this new phase, I believe, will involve conscious choices about community and linking local communities to the global community in enriching ways. A great part of our mission at the Institute of Noetic Sciences (IONS) is to engage global community, recognizing the importance of nurturing local groups as individual nodes of the global learning community through content, materials and networking capacities. Together we're exploring one of the most fundamental questions of our time: What will it take for us to move into a worldview, or into a set of worldviews, that can allow for the appreciation of difference such that we can reduce conflicts?

IONS was founded in 1973 by Edgar Mitchell, one of the Apollo 14 astronauts. He had what he described as "the window seat" on the way home, and was able to look out on the planet Earth from the vantage point of deep space and see it as a whole system, in its pristine beauty, suspended in the larger universe. His experience was two-fold. One the one hand, he despaired that the state of human consciousness was creating most (if not all) of the problems we face as a civilization, and that we were focusing in the wrong direction—outside ourselves, rather than inside ourselves. At the same time, he experienced a real epiphany, a moment of joy and ecstasy in which he found himself fundamentally connected with all of the universe, recognizing the fundamental nature of *unity*. So here he was, an MIT-trained scientist, a person of one paradigm suddenly experiencing something he had never known or predicted. Mitchell came back to Earth as a seeker; he returned between stories, searching for ways to turn the outward lens of the Apollo space program into an Apollo program of inner space.

For many years, IONS has been fulfilling that mission, mobilizing the resources and intention of the collective in order to understand and appreciate the complexities of consciousness and inner experience. Using the discernment and rigor of science, we ask new questions that propel us toward new answers about the human condition and the powers and potentials that lie within us for greatness, for unity, for mutual appreciation and for our fullness as collaborators on planet Earth. As we move into this new decade, IONS is poised to offer our greatest contribution to advancing the science of noetic experience in order to promote collective well-being. We do this by engaging the world through a Global Engagement Initiative and our Global Community Group Network, by translating our archives into educational materials for youth, scientists and anyone interested in learning more about consciousness—and through many other programs and pursuits.

It's not just materialist science proving faith; it's how science and the religious and spiritual traditions can come together in mutual respect to learn and explore the fullness of our human potentials. We *do* have extraordinary powers as human beings—to do destruction and harm, or to facilitate the growth of this beautiful garden and live into our evolutionary agency, able to bridge our differences into the next story.

For three decades, scientist and anthropologist Marilyn Mandala Schlitz, PhD, has pioneered clinical and field-based research in the area of human consciousness, transformation and healing. She is a thought leader on matters of individual and social change whose respected voice offers new insights into the most pressing challenges of our time. A researcher, speaker, change consultant and writer, Marilyn is the author of Living Deeply: The Art and Science of Transformation in Everyday Life *and* Consciousness and Healing: Integral Approaches to Mind Body Medicine.

Marilyn serves as the CEO and President of the Institute of Noetic Sciences (IONS), where she has worked for fifteen years. She is also Senior Scientist at the California Pacific Medical Center. Noetic science is featured prominently in the novel by Dan Brown, The Lost Symbol. *Please visit www.Noetic.org and www.MarilynSchlitz.com for further information. You can also follow Marilyn and IONS happenings on Twitter: www.Twitter.com/MarilynSchlitz.*

Dr. Christine Page

2012: RETURN OF THE GREAT MOTHER

To the Maya and many other ancient people, our galaxy, the Milky Way, is seen as the Great Mother who gives birth to our earthly life and to whom our soul will eventually return.

The center of the galaxy is known as the Heart of the Great Mother, and it is believed that through this portal, a far greater heart (known by many cultures as the central sun of the central sun) can be accessed. Within this heart lies the ocean of possibilities, the eternal source of all existence. At present, our sun is experiencing a unique twenty-six-thousand-year alignment with the galactic center, allowing us to access and personify a level of expanded consciousness beyond any ever seen on Earth before.

To make the most of this extraordinary opportunity, we must align our heart to the Heart of the Mother through the acceptance of her three faces: Virgin, Mother and Crone—all of which exist within our own psyche. Only then can we create a new world worthy of the generations to come, one of peace and unity through appreciation of diversity and our eternal nature.

This passage of the sun across the galactic center, due to conclude towards 2020, takes approximately thirty-six years. During this period of time, we are primarily under the control of the Crone aspect of the Great Mother, dying to old beliefs and patterns so that we can make way for and embody the showers of high frequency cosmic rays now entering our atmosphere from the galactic center.

In other words, we are dissolving to evolve. To deepen our understanding of this process, let us study the breath, a natural and essential process for every human being. The word *inspiration* means to breathe life into something and is closely related to the virginal quality of the Great Mother. The archetypal energy of the Virgin holds within our heart our spiritual blueprint, which expresses the reason

> *Love connects us to our wholeness, helping us to remember who we truly are.*

for our existence, our soul's destiny. The Virgin's greatest pleasure is to inspire us to follow our dreams, bringing what was just an idea plucked from the ocean of possibilities into manifestation. She speaks to us through our intuition, urging us on when we lack enthusiasm, shining a light when we appear to be lost. She commonly speaks to us through our night dreams, when the veils between dimensions are thin and we are more receptive to the possibility of change.

Her purpose is to connect us to our wholeness, using the power of love that emanates from the center of the heart. She does not judge our creations, as she knows all ideas emerge from the womb of the Great Mother. However, the Virgin will lovingly encourage us to recognize patterns of behavior which nurture our soul and those which don't, asking us the question: *What am I doing from love and what from fear, shame or guilt?*

Love connects us to our wholeness, helping us to remember who we truly are. As we continue our hero's journey to see the seed of our idea become manifest and blossom as a mighty tree, the Mother energy of Great Mother steps forward, nurturing our journey by providing us with suitable gifts and talents. Such nourishment is unique to each of us but can easily be buried when not kept alight through encouragement and support.

Knowing this to be a potential challenge, the Mother also will send us mentors—men and women who enter our life, especially when we are young—to surround us in love, encourage our dreams and mirror our own potential. Like Gandalf or Merlin within modern mythology, most mentors stay with us for just a short time before departing, leaving a deep impression of our soul's potential stored within our cellular memory. It is important for all of us to recognize these mentors. I encourage each of you to look back on your life, describe the qualities of your mentors and then ask: *Where are these qualities being expressed in my life today? Am I fully using the gifts and talents handed down to me by the Great Mother when I was born?*

At this extraordinary time in our history, the transformative energies available are allowing every soul to be fully expressed in its divine form. This is why there are so many beings on this planet today. You were one of the lucky ones; you had a winning lottery ticket. However, it is one thing to turn up and another matter to be present to the choices being offered. Once we understand that we have been and always will be creators of our reality and not victims of some higher authority, we can appreciate that everything around us is a reflection of our spiritual blueprint, beliefs and intentionality.

> *At this extraordinary time in our history, the transformative energies available are allowing every soul to be fully expressed in its divine form.*

The questions we need to ask ourselves are these: *Am I being true to myself? Am I being authentic? Where have I become a victim of my own created reality? What is master of my creative energy, my head or my heart? Are the beliefs of my mind in alignment with the desires of my heart?* We cannot make choices to change our life while we blame others for its creation or are ashamed of its appearance. Love and acceptance are the only answers.

Now we seek the guidance of the Crone. Like the Virgin, she knows and holds our spiritual blueprint close to her heart. And yet, while the Virgin is seen as the creator, the Crone is the destroyer. She is the one who loves us so much that she will tear down beliefs and stories that no longer serve us, even though we suffer feelings of grief and despair as the structures that gave us security disappear. The Crone's fiery energy dissolves the physical structure of the caterpillar until only the liquefied contents of the cocoon remain, for the Crone knows the butterfly that waits within. Our world is going through such a transition, inevitably leading to fear and anxiety as the old is destroyed and the new is still un-manifest. But remember, the heart knows the truth, and it guides us towards the abundance waiting within the heart of the Great Mother.

The so-called "end of time" also belongs to the Crone, for the linear paradigm of time embracing a past, present and future is dissolving, returning us to cyclical time wherein we live in the center of a circle of our experiences, all of which exist in the same moment. It takes great courage to allow our own inner Crone to take control of our life. Our will, pride or arrogance often hold tightly to their creations, forgetting that we were meant to create only in order to nurture the collective consciousness of the Great Mother.

I am sure we all remember a time when we were working on a jigsaw puzzle and, despite their obvious disparity, forced two pieces of the puzzle together. Then, ignoring our higher wisdom, we proceeded to build the rest of the jigsaw around these mismatched pieces, creating stories upon stories, all emerging from fear, guilt or shame of the original "sin."

Yet one day, through love of self and under the guidance of the Crone, we courageously face the truth and tear the puzzle down to its original parts—recognizing there are no mistakes, just a willingness to evolve. To achieve such a transformation, we must choose at this time to express our unique spiritual blueprint and shine forth, like a flower, with all our petals (aspects of the soul) fully open. This alchemical process is achieved through full embodiment of the soul within our physical form and the beautiful planet Earth. The greatest challenge is to recognize which of our petals are still closed and which have been disowned due to shame or fear (usually relating to issues of power).

Now is the time to recognize and accept into the heart all aspects of the self so we will know wholeness. The easiest way of recognizing dispossessed parts is to observe where we project our judgments and fears, knowing that where we have an emotional reaction to another person, a part of us awaits acceptance.

> *Yet one day, through love of self and under the guidance of the Crone, we courageously face the truth and tear the puzzle down to its original parts—recognizing there are no mistakes, just a willingness to evolve.*

The Crone controls this second stage of the breath: expiration, when we die to the old in order to give birth to the new, completing the cycle of breath and bringing heaven onto earth and earth into heaven. Many Western cultures give little acknowledgement to the importance of the out-breath, often expressing a great fear of death and a desire to maintain outward appearances at any cost. From my medical perspective, this can lead to a propensity to illnesses such as asthma, dementia, heart disease and hormonal disturbances, as many of the physiological functions of the body are based on a harmony maintained through two equal and opposite forces working together. Fortunately, nature surrounds us with this message through the annual seasons, the movement of waves and the cycles of the moon.

When we look at the moon, we tend to notice the light in the night sky rather than the accompanying darkness; together, however, they create a circle. At the start of the cycle, there is just a circle of darkness seen as the mother moon. Within a day, she has given birth to that sliver of silvery light we call a new moon. Over time the dark mother shrinks as the light develops into a full moon. Now the light fills the circle, reflecting the complete manifestation of our idea (which we call success).

Yet this is only half of the moon's monthly cycle—for as the moon waxes, the son who has been crowned king must agree to die, feeding the dark mother with his successes so that she expands. Eventually, at the full moon, he unites with her completely; giving her his seed before he dies and leaving us with a night of darkness.

But never fear: the moon is a divine gift from the Mother, reminding us that out of the darkness will come a new moon; out of the cocoon will come the beautiful butterfly; out of the death of the old world will come a new and beautiful planet of peace and joy.

Christine Page's upbringing was somewhat unusual, immersed as she was within metaphysical exploration and energy healing. From her birth, near London, England, she maintained her intuitive connection to other dimensions and today is seen as a gifted intuitive and mystic. Qualifying as a doctor from London University in 1978, she used this inner wisdom in her work as a physician within both orthodox and complementary medicine. In 1997, she left her healing and homeopathic practice to concentrate on helping others to connect to the feminine aspects of their being through intuition, nurturing and renewal. For the past twelve years she has taught internationally, using mythology, alchemy and astrology to realign individuals to their hearts—knowing that it is through the heart that they accept the expanded levels of consciousness reaching our planet at this time.

Christine is the author of six books. Her latest, 2012 and the Galactic Center: The Return of the Great Mother, is a synthesis of her inner teachings. It reveals that during this monumental alignment, we are being offered the opportunity to know wholeness and health at a whole new level, as perfected human beings. She and her husband, Leland, run unique astrology seminars, week-long retreats and sacred tours from their base in Northern California. www.ChristinePage. com

Mark Borax

SPRINGING THE SOUL
OF A STUCK SPECIES

Species mutation. Planetary upheaval. Cosmic shift. As you push on earning a living, raising a family, juggling the never-ending details of daily existence, what's the relevance of these earthshaking predictions? How does cosmic shift relate to ordinary life? What does 2012 mean to you and me?

In twenty-two years as a soul level astrologer, I've learned prophecies become true *when we make them true*. At any given time, more than one future forms up ahead, complicating the business of prediction. Each of us has a role to play in drawing the optimal future out of less desirable outcomes. When you factor in everyone on Earth who is likely to have a say in what's about to happen regarding 2012, it becomes clear that a large part of prophecy hinges on free will.

So, in order to draw in the optimal future, what should we do with our free will? We can make an intention, now, to pry ourselves out of the past and open ourselves to something much different. This is harder than it sounds. It's easy to idolize cosmic metamorphosis written in a book. But to knead these truths into the stuff of your life each day—that's the way to bring on the future. Anything less has already been tried at one time or other throughout history. Through the ages, great masters have given us higher truths that we haven't been able to sustain.

The one thing left is to try believing in ourselves—try on the idea that humanity was never meant to suffer and struggle in an endless limbo of epic proportions, but to fulfill its bright potential as a species—and get on with something that matters. To pull this off, we need a clear picture of what we're coming out of and going into. Prophecies, in other words, require volunteers. 2012 is offering the world a marvelous opportunity to cut through illusion and get to something real.

> *So, in order to draw in the optimal future,*
> *what should we do with our free will?*

As a visionary seer, trained mystic, astrologer and shaman, I've learned that the simple fact that these things were prophesied once upon a time doesn't let us off the hook. If anything, it puts us on the spot even more. It provides a job description. Destiny is a product of collaboration between human beings and higher cosmic forces. No ancient prophecy is going to force change upon us. Your destiny is always streaming toward you like a tangible but invisible force—but in order for it to happen, you've got to stream toward it; you've got to take it up willingly. Only when you've exhausted every means to make higher truth real can you meet the prophecies where they need to be met if they're going to take root and change the world.

Prophecies have many, various interpretations. You've got to make ancient codes your own; take them to heart; test them against the rigors of the current moment. Making cosmic prophecy real is like building a home or writing a book—you start with a broad, sweeping vision. Then you bleed and sweat over that vision moment by moment until you get so far into it that you create the reality.

Another principle that ought to be considered is human nature's stubborn resistance to change. The closer we get to an actual different living future, the more resistance is aroused, throwing everything into chaos. The old fears the new, which heralds its demise. As the new inches closer to the present, the old freaks out, vying for dominance, insinuating that the collective dream of love, peace and understanding is a hallucination left over from the 1960s. This clash between old and new, progressive and retrogressive, is not just relegated to our society, but happens within ourselves as well. In each of us, hunger for change drives us forward while fear holds us back. It's always dangerous breaking new ground. Our face gets squashed against invisible taboos that paralyze our species. In reaction, society yanks us back into the apparent safety of old, insane ways.

So, how can we each use this momentous world timing of 2012 to bring cosmic shift all the way in? How can we change in a way that sticks? I see 2012 as a massive planetary death and rebirth. The life we've been living since the heyday of capitalism, that Dickensian world we inherited from Mr. Scrooge, is expiring. A high-tech, amped-up, global society that keeps its species in bondage, teaching

> *We stayed so long at the masquerade ball that we got stuck in our masks.*

children to betray themselves to make a buck, is bankrupt. A world culture that consumes and consumes with no regard for the future is collapsing all around us. That is what's dying.

What's being born, in its earliest stage, is a new sense of purpose for our species. In recent centuries, humanity lost its purpose. We've forgotten who we are. Fake security became the idol we worship. We sold our souls to buy a massive hoax that adores the outer at the expense of the inner. We stuffed our truth in return for an artificial existence that has run out of steam.

We stayed so long at the masquerade ball that we got stuck in our masks. We confused our true selves with perky little consumers of a now-bankrupt ideology, conscientious little soldiers of the market-place. In place of deep aliveness and radical joy, we substituted the toxic mentality of tabloid gossip and TV sitcoms. The world became one big shopping mall. Amidst such an epidemic of delusion, it *would* take something as big as planetary crisis to pry us out of illusion and get us back on track. The track now opening is a pathway back to a life that counts, a love that matters, a world that pays attention to what's real rather than the canned laughter of vicarious existence.

Somewhere along the line, we got so twisted that we now have to untwist and come back to the simple daily rapture of beingness, the great gift of being alive in a miraculous, ever-changing universe. A lot of garbage that got laid over this basic human right has to be purged from world consciousness. It's a time of great upheaval, inner and outer.

The road opening now is a road that started to open many times throughout history and got diverted. We gave our power to churches and priests, presidents and prime ministers, TV screens and tabloids. We've misplaced our greatness. We've come to see ourselves in a puny, distorted mirror. Even if everybody doesn't recognize the tremendous opportunity being offered to us at this time, people sense on a gut level that our civilization has rushed to the edge of a perilous cliff, with no option at all to keep going the same blind way. Our jobs, our lives and our loves must be purged of bullshit.

How many of us walk through the world on fire? Who reaches to grasp their dream instead of putting it off for that famous "someday?" How many live the life they were born to? How long are you going to keep swallowing your truth to fit into a broken world? As we approach 2012, more and more people will ask themselves these questions, as a wave of collective transformation gains critical mass. Despite our resistance to change, change has arrived. Despite our allergy to truth, truth is bursting out. Look at the eyes of babies fresh to the world, filled with holy wonder for this juicy, blue-green body of the goddess we inhabit. What would it be like for you to be that alive at your age, inside your skin? What would it be to burn that bright and build a life around it?

Do you know you are a vast, limitless, cosmic entity who became human specifically at one place in time to get something done that only you can do? Do you know you are a *Giant of Love* whose soul is packed with enough power to steer the universe?

I see 2012 as a *crisis of meaning,* designed to ignite, throughout the globe, a common hunger in each human soul to clear away the junk world and rebuild this place from the ground up, based on a few simple truths. Regardless of who you are, where you live, how much money you make or whether you're lucky or unlucky in love; despite the trash that media mouths and political pundits spout every day as truth, in every corner of every country people are—against the odds—awakening.

> If you put your ear to the ground, you'll hear it rumbling in the soul of the species: the coming of the new.

Each week, in my job counseling individuals by phone, I feel this force building. I feel it in my own impatience to stay stuck in old behavior patterns that hold the future at bay. I feel the impulse for change conquering the inertia and apathy that is our peculiar burden in history.

If you put your ear to the ground, you'll hear it rumbling in the soul of the species: the coming of the new. Out of the debris of the past, a new Earth is rising. It's not easy, at first, to distinguish it from the old. You've got to feel your way in. You can't take anybody else's word for it. You can't use old maps and rulebooks. You can't afford to sleepwalk through this changing of the guard. You've got to find, someplace deep inside yourself, this cosmic transformation we're all talking about.

In the old world, we stood watching societal leaders point to the sky and say, "Down," and we said, *"Down."* In the old world, we watched authority figures point to the ground and say, "Up," and we said *"Up."* That world fed its children into a machine that eats soul in the name of profit while spewing toxic waste: *Just go with the program a little further. Don't make waves.* Just turn on the TV, eat your synthetic corn, and it'll be all right.

Amidst life as usual, here in the hectic first decade of the twenty-first century, flickering across ring tones and computer screens, buzzing through sound bytes along the information highway, pounding out a subversive tribal drumbeat, can you sense a new world art emerging, the creative urge to be done with lies and get on with something *real?*

Civilization is a karmic wound bleeding in order to heal. History is a spent snakeskin hooked on a cactus so the snake can wriggle free. Everything wrong with our world is an abrasive surface for us to scrape against, stripping away the sugar-coated lies our elders told us; shedding mass delusion; rubbing ourselves newborn, raw, primal, alive from within as lusty, intimate lovers with this thrumming world goddess, who, ancient and nubile, rises from the steamy jungle and opens her core to receive us into the alchemical crucible of gut-level transformation.

What is your job description? How will you honor the celestial DNA of your blueprint on Earth? Will you collaborate with cosmic forces to bring about the spring of the soul? Each of us has come here for a reason unique to us. Each of us is here to flower from the root, to dig down into the fertile soil of our inner nature and base a life on that. Don't take my word for it. Don't hold back. Don't piss away another incarnation. Make it yours.

Who are you really? What are you here to do? How much longer are you going to wait?

Mark Borax is a nomadic poet, soul astrologer and bestselling author. In the mid-eighties, Mark began two pivotal relationships that would shape his life and career: he was befriended by the idol of his adolescence, writer Ray Bradbury, who became his literary godfather, and by teacher and visionary astrologer Ellias Lonsdale, with whom he apprenticed for seven years. Ellias and Mark founded a mystery school in northern California, birthing a new form of astrology: Star Genesis.

Mark created Soul Level Astrology in 1987, and has since helped thousands of people identify and claim their life purpose using the birth chart as a window to the soul. Mark's first book, 2012: Crossing the Bridge to the Future, *tells the story of his apprenticeship with Ellias and describes how 2012 is an evolutionary gateway to a transformative future. His second book,* Cosmic Weather Report: Guidance for Radically Changing Times, *will be out in December, 2010 (Frog Books and Random House). Mark founded the College of Visionaries and Wizards, which offers the mystery school described in his book via live teleclasses. He lives in Vermont with his wife Marcella Eversole and their sons. To learn more about Mark, visit www.MarkBorax.com.*

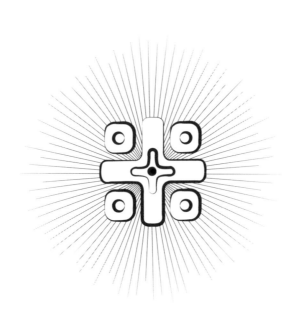

Elizabeth Jenkins

THE RETURN OF THE INKA

Something dawns
Golden
Warm and spreading
A spiritual nectar
At once sublime and earthly

Instinctively
We turn toward it
Intoxicating
Irresistible
Startling in its beauty
Completely natural
Supernatural

We face into it
Receive its smooth force
Soft, relentless
Slowly washing over the world
Polishing, renewing
Revealing to us what has always
  been there

As familiar and alien
As our own unignited DNA
A gift as yet unopened
A treasure unexplored
The hand of God held out to us
Our own hand
Filled with promise

The Return of the Inka (the Quechua prefer this spelling) is a prophecy that has been preserved for us thanks to the Q'ero Indians of Peru—the modern-day descendants of the Inka—and anthropologist Juan Nunez del Prado. Juan says that in January 1990, Don Manuel Q'espi, one of the most powerful Andean Masters of the Q'ero Nation, came to his house early in the morning wearing his most splendid ceremonial garb. He had walked all the way from Q'ero to tell Juan that he had seen the signs in the mountains—the time of the prophecy was at hand. After the "cosmic reordering" period, from 1990 to 1993, the first phases of the prophecy would begin and could potentially reach culmination in the year 2012.

The Inka Empire, possibly the largest sub-continental empire on Earth, had one of the best systems for the gathering and redistribution of resources (in other words, one of the best social security systems) the world has ever known. There was no hunger, no unemployment and no poverty. The Sapa Inka and Sapa Qoya (high King and Queen) were experts in social engineering, agriculture, the arts— and, of course, spiritual matters. The Sapa Inkas and Qoyas were Priest-Kings and Priest-Queens who revered nature as their greatest teacher.

The Inkan prophecy carried down through the lineage of Sapa Inkas and Qoyas to modern times is actually a kind of map that not only reveals something of such tantamount importance as our own spiritual heritage, but also marks the pathway to our very future— complete with road signs—for the potential evolution of the human race.

The Inkas' wisdom rivals modern physics in its understanding of the world as living energy; but, unlike modern physics, the Inkas evolved a highly sophisticated, yet simple, set of spiritual tools teaching us how to interact with, and even direct, the flows of this world of living energies. First, the cosmo-vision of the Inkas reminds us who we are as human beings. Their wisdom holds that, contrary to modern Judeo-Christian thought, we are born from *original virtue,* not original sin. We can therefore trust ourselves, and know that we live in an overabundant cosmos that is full of life rather than inert matter.

According to the Inka, we inhabit a living universe called *Kausay Pacha,* "world of living energy," a world in which everyone and indeed every*thing* is alive and has consciousness. In this overabundant universe, Pachamama—Mother Earth—is a generous, fecund and loving mother. We are only able to grow and develop our "Inka seed," the potential in every person, with the help of this loving mother.

The Inka posit seven levels of what we would call "psycho-spiritual development" which lie dormant within our "Inka seed." The spiritual tools of the Inka help us unfold each level of our development in an organic succession. While the first three levels consist of a kind of spiritual childhood and adolescence, it is at the fourth-level initiation that one takes one's first steps toward becoming a true "adult."

> *We are only able to grow and develop our "Inka seed," the potential in every person, with the help of this loving mother.*

At each level, the initiate gains an ever-widening sense of identity with larger and larger human groups, as well as a correlating ability to resonate their personal "bubble," aura or energy field with ever increasing areas of geography, or Pachamama. For example, at the first level you identify with your immediate family, local town and accompanying nature beings—the spirits of the local mountains, lakes or rivers. At the second level you identify with your state or province including the environment, and at the third level you identify yourself with your country and the spirit of its highest mountain, or biggest river or ocean.

At the fourth level initiation (which traditionally takes place inside an ancient cave in Peru) you become able to resonate your energetic field with the entire field of living energy that is Mother Earth and her inhabitants. This is the level at which every other human being literally becomes your brother or your sister because you have the same mother, Pachamama, and the same father, Inti Tayta, Father Sun. The next three levels delineate the unfolding of the complete potential of humankind right up to the seventh level at which a human may become fully vested with creative power, manifest "the equivalent of God on Earth," and resonate with the energy field of the entire universe.

Most of us are considered to have barely arrived to the third level or perhaps to be teetering on the edge of the fourth level. Fear, conflict, dependence on authority and victimization are the hallmarks of the third level. Harmony, independence, happiness and self-direction are the hallmarks of the fourth. The simplest way to proceed in one's spiritual growth is through direct, conscious cooperation with the living energies of Mother Nature.

The fourth-level initiate takes on the responsibility to become an active participant not only in the creation of his own life, but also in the unfolding of the Inka prophecy, as this prophecy requires our active participation. The wisdom of the fourth level holds that in our abundant, life-filled universe there is no such thing as positive or negative energy; there are only relatively heavier energies, *hoocha,* and relatively finer energies, *sami. Sami,* in the Quechua language of the Inka, means "nectar." It is literally a spiritual food that we as humans endowed with free will, can choose to create and to channel, or not.

All of nature produces *sami.* Think of how you instinctively want

> *The simplest way to proceed in one's spiritual growth is through direct, conscious cooperation with the living energies of Mother Nature.*

to go out for a walk when you feel out of sorts. Only we humans produce *hoocha.* But as the generators of heavy energies we are also equipped with the capacity to direct living energy and to "eat and digest" or transmute *hoocha.* When we become initiates of the fourth level in this ancient spiritual tradition of the Andes, we develop an ever-increasing capacity to direct and channel the flow of *sami,* the finest living energy, and to absorb and redirect heavy energy to Pachamama—the place where it can become useful as kind of spiritual compost. Certainly without our sacred reciprocity of breathing with trees and plants our lives would soon be extinguished.

It is the sharing that is important. It is the sharing that makes our next step in evolution possible, if and only if humans and nature can cooperate to create the conditions to make the leap to the next level, the fifth level. The spiritual cosmo-vision of the Q'ero holds precious, even life-saving, information for today's world. The perspective of the fourth-level teachings offers a way out of the many woes of modern society. For example, the fourth-level teachings can forever end the "war between the sexes" by providing a personal experience of male and female as complementary and harmonious living energies.

> *It is the sharing that is important.*

The fourth level can offer new perspectives to those who think only in terms of "good" and "bad," and give legs to the modern "new age movement" that often promotes philosophies of escape from earthly existence, when our salvation is right here in front of us encoded in our very physiology, and in Mother Nature. The most exciting thing is that once enough of us truly step on the path of the fourth level, together and in cooperation with Mother Nature, we can create the conditions for one of us to break through to the fifth level and become a master healer as the prophecies tell us is our potential.

According to the prophecies, the first fifth-level healer is due to appear anytime at an Ice Festival on top of a glacier in Peru. This festival represents a huge gathering of human beings (over seventy thousand people) participating in a sacred ritual (producing loads of *sami*) at a powerful sacred site (on top of an ice peak) in cooperation with a powerful force of nature, the mountain spirit known as Apu Sinak'ara. It is precisely this collaboration of human living energy with a great force of nature (the ice peak) that provides the energetic "womb" from which the fifth-level healer/priest can emerge. The prophecy states that all twelve healers will emerge in connection with sacred festivals that take place all over Peru at different times of the year. The Q'ollorit'I (Ice) Festival, for example, takes place at the last full moon in May or first full moon in June every year. Don Benito Qoriwaman, a famous Andean healer and keeper of the full prophecy, once told a student that a fifth-level initiate could walk into the United Nations, and by their presence alone, transform every human interaction of conflict into a solution session.

The "Return of the Inka" prophesies the emergence of sixth-level initiates—truly enlightened leaders—who cooperate with nature to lead us into a golden era for humanity. Following the laws of this organic spiritual tradition, we know the path to higher consciousness lies in resonating with ever larger aspects of Mother Nature. It is curious that December 21, 2012, marks a perfect alignment of our Earth, sun and galactic center. The Inka prophecies say this energy doorway stands open since the priests first saw the signs in 1990. Whether or not we seize this opportunity to harmonize ourselves with what Mother Nature is offering, is up to each one of us. *Who will step through this doorway with me? Will you step through?*

———————————

Elizabeth B. Jenkins, MA, MFCC, is a licensed psychotherapist and author of two books on the Inka mystical tradition. The international bestseller The Return of the Inka: A Journey of Initiation *and* Inka Prophecies for 2012, *originally published as* Initiation, *was published in twenty countries. Her most recent book is* Journey To Q'eros: Golden Cradle of the Inka.

Elizabeth has taught the spiritual tools of the Inka worldwide, and led trips to Peru to experience the fourth-level initiation of the Inka for the past twenty years. She lives on an organic orchard in Hawaii where she offers special trainings and programs with the Q'ero Indians of Peru. She is also a singer-songwriter and produced the CD Inka Spirit. *Elizabeth founded Wiraqocha Foundation for the Preservation of Indigenous Wisdom in 1996, and collaborates with native Hawaiian kahuna, healers and teachers, as well as the fantastic forces of Mother Nature on the Big Island of Hawaii. To learn more about Elizabeth, visit www.Inka-Online.com.*

Gregory Hoag

THE SACRED GEOMETRIC KEYS TO 2012

Every aspect of this reality reflects the creative, energetic impulse from Source through geometry. From the microscopic to the galactic, energy organizes and expresses itself in the physical dimension through geometry. We don't perceive the underlying energy directly, and thus describe all matter through the geometric patterns it expresses. Still, we must recognize that matter follows precise energetic templates that precede it, as a metal mold receives warm Jell-O, which takes on the mold's shape as it cools or lowers its energetic vibratory rate. This aspect of reality has been demonstrated using Kirlian photography, which shows the full energetic image of a leaf after some lobes are cut away in the physical dimension.

The Maya reflected these higher energetic archetypes directly, in both their pyramids and the construction of their calendar. By so doing, they were able to create a resonance with the higher dimensions, the Divine. This is similar to the way in which a "C" tuning fork will start to vibrate in rhythm with a "C" tone. Thus they brought the human, physical dimension into resonance with the Divine and transformed their level of being.

Scientists define our reality as the way in which space and time interact as two different dimensional patterns (the space/time continuum). The Maya used these same formulating aspects in the construction of their calendar (i.e., geometric patterns and interacting cycles of time). They considered the architect of the universe to be Hunab K'u, meaning "the One Giver of Movement and Measure" (time and space), the Absolute Being, the center of the Galaxy. Pacal Votan, the great Mayan avatar of the seventh century, taught: "All is number. God is number. God is in all." He shared that "we are intimately linked with and informed by the galaxy. All of life is ordered by the same re-occurring patterns."

The message from the Maya is: We are spiritual/multi-dimensional beings who have chosen to incarnate into physical density at this unique time so that we might learn, grow and, most importantly, take advantage of the 2012 timing to expand the flow of love and consciousness into our lives and the Earth. Our greatest opportunity is to evolve spiritually, as we embody higher dimensional energies that will transform this reality, expanding Source into third-dimensional density and literally raising the vibration of matter.

The Maya, who created their calendar thousands of years ago, were not invested in 2012 per se. They were interested in their daily lives, and the yearly progression of their well-being—as we all are. 2012 was not their prophetic cry to the end of time, but rather their calendar anchor point defining the transition of Earth's greatest cycle. They identified the fifty-two-thousand-year cosmic day of the Earth's energetic progression through each of the twelve signs of the zodiac. It takes two complete cycles because a day is twenty-four hours with each hour (one through twelve) visited twice, once in the light and once in the dark.

The Earth is now moving from the night side of this long cycle, with December 2012 marking our energetic alignment with the core of our galaxy as the beginning of a new cosmic day. Using the proper geometric patterns to overlay this time cycle, the Maya reverse-engineered a calendar into their time frame that gave them one of the more powerful divining tools for deciphering and grounding the space/time continuum and its effects on Earth's evolution. Why they chose 2012, and how they configured its regression into their time, are essential questions facing us today. To understand is to discover our human potential and develop a map for our future evolution.

When the proper geometries are chosen and aligned with the correct time cycles, vibrations are generated that are resonant with the essence of all existence. The combination of these select cycles and geometries are referred to as sacred when they create relationship with the Divine. The Maya could foresee the manifestation of divine rhythms by interpreting their patterned time cycles. The gift they were offered was that, by following these sacred pathways, they could learn to open a conduit through the many dimensions separating human beings from Source—Hunab K'u—allowing for a flow of divine transformative energy.

> *Why they chose 2012, and how they configured its regression into their time, are essential questions facing us today. To understand is to discover our human potential and develop a map for our future evolution.*

Higher-dimensional energy flow is a critical concept to understand, not only for deciphering the motivation behind the Mayan calendar, but more importantly for uncovering the opportunity now present as the energies of 2012 embrace us. There are many dimensions that permeate our reality. Ordinary physical senses do not readily perceive these dimensions, which are made distinct from each other, in part, by differences in vibrational frequency. People who see auras or have near-death experiences are interacting with these coexisting dimensions. Our root (soul) exists at the highest level of frequency available to us while in physical form. The density of the dimension we inhabit, as well as the many dimensions between the physical and Source, inhibits energy flow. The rapid increase of toxin-producing technologies, electromagnetic pollution, negative emotions and mental stress also block higher-dimensional energy flow. Our health, happiness and very existence depend on this flow of energy into our daily lives. When it is blocked, disease and all difficulties occur.

Recent theories on evolution have postulated that a radical change can occur almost instantaneously, rather than slowly, over eons. A necessary component of this is a large energy influx, which describes what we are now moving through with Earth's involvement with the galactic core. Our sun is seen as a lens, or focuser, of the galactic core. Twice a year, it aligns with these energies, but a higher level of core pulsation is occurring at this transition time. 2012 is prophesied to be the height or middle of this energy surge.

Our health, happiness and very existence depend on this flow of energy into our daily lives. When it is blocked, disease and all difficulties occur.

One way NASA has measured this change is by monitoring Earth's electromagnetic field via a project called Themis. They have found that the field has expanded greatly in size, reducing its density and thus its ability to shield the planet from bombardments of solar and cosmic energy flows as it has for eons. A direct result is an increased flow of this energy into our planet, and consequently into the electromagnetic field (aura) of our bodies as well. People are being forced into a higher rate of action and change by this influx of energy.

What this means for each of us is demonstrated by this example: To transform a block of ice, it takes the input of energy, in the form of heat, to create water. Add more energy and the water is transformed into a gas. Likewise, the increased energy of the galactic alignment is already showing up in our lives, forcing transformation on many levels. The difficulties lie in all the blockages in our energy field, created predominantly by fear, toxins and electromagnetic pollution. The emotional, mental and physical aspects of our being are feeling the increased pressure of this pent-up vibrational energy. We are faced with a choice: either breakdown and devolution or breakthrough and spiritual evolution. If we accept this flow of higher consciousness, the dysfunctional parts of our personality and culture can be recognized and released, leaving us open to our true potential: enlightenment in divine love.

As we personally transform, so goes the world. This is an extraordinary and potentially wonderful time to be alive, and yet a very challenging process. We require support and tools to get us through this transition. Through my study and work over the last thirty-eight years, I have rediscovered Sacred Geometric forms that offer some of the most powerful tools to effect positive change in people's lives. These sacred forms are the most ancient and effective transceivers of higher dimensional energy in the physical dimension. A tool can be necessary and empowering—like a hammer that allows you to build a house. When you're finished, *you've* built the house, not the hammer. Yet you wouldn't be able to create the house without the hammer. We need all the support we can garner as we face an overload of blockages and the breakdown of old paradigms, and as the accelerating energy input of the 2012 cycle drives this blessed transformation.

As we personally transform, so goes the world.

The Mayan calendar is an important tool pointing toward the increased speed of our present life experience. As put forth by Carl Johan Calleman in his book, *The Mayan Calendar and the Transformation of Consciousness*, the Maya used a time system that can be extrapolated back to the birth of our universe. This system is broken into day and night periods as well as heaven and underworld components of increasing fractal units. Their calendar displays the patterns and rhythms of evolution with a complexity only recently discovered by modern scientists. Calleman also demonstrated that evolution and time events are accelerating in exponential factors of twenty as we approach the transition point of 2012. The success of the Mayan calendar is unmistakeable, the geometric roots of its construction a mystery to unravel.

We currently base our perception of time on the cycle of Earth's rotation on its axis, and its larger cycle around the sun. Unfortunately, this has little relationship to greater evolutionary cycles. Time itself is an agreed-upon construct with little intrinsic meaning. The Mayan method of time measurement worked on such a large divine scale because it was merged with Sacred Geometric constructs to give it relational substance to physical reality. The Maya geometrized time.

All components of the Mayan calendar, and even the 2012 date in the Gregorian calendar that we use today, have Sacred Geometric roots and metaphors because each component of God's fractal universe is always filled with purpose, meaning and symbol. Our opportunity is to discover and apply these keys to 2012. This will not only give us a deeper understanding of creation, but it will also support us in our next steps to construct the "tools" needed in this time of deep transformation—a time of potential ascension.

One of today's foremost Mayan elders, Hunbatz Men, has referred to Gregory Hoag as "the most knowledgeable teacher of Sacred Geometry that I have encountered." As a scientist and artist, Gregory has researched Sacred Geometry and consciousness for thirty-eight years. Following a major energetic awakening (Kundalini) in 1982, he started communicating with higher dimensional beings and offering energetic tools through Metaforms Ltd. He was first introduced to the Mayan calendar in 1987 as he and his wife, Gail, along with several others, met weekly with José Argüelles while searching for a way to introduce the world to Harmonic Convergence. Gregory works with Archangel Metatron to foster spiritual evolution and the expansion of Source. His land in the Colorado Rockies is dedicated to the purpose of activating the planetary grid and energetic vortexes. He is recognized as one of the leading experts on Sacred Geometric tools for improving health, raising consciousness, reducing stress, manifesting intent and clearing emotional and electromagnetic interference. To learn more, visit www.MetaForms.net.

Sri Ram Kaa and Kira Raa

2012: THE MOMENT OF TRUTH

Over seventy years ago, Gandhi stated: *"An error does not become truth by reason of multiplied propagation, nor does truth become error because nobody sees it."* Our world has arrived at its moment of truth. That critical point of reckoning clearly demonstrates that structures based upon models of antiquity are releasing and new paradigms are coming forward. This brings forward a challenge to those of us who are navigating a human life experience. Are we ready to fully embrace our Self-Ascended truth?

This is the time for reunification—on every level. Between North and South, eagle and condor, man and woman, ego and spirit. We have arrived at the moment when everyone is offered the chance to transcend the limited egoic-mind and reunite with the soul at the heart of creation.

Our own Sacred Reunion occurred seven years ago. While hiking together in the Sedona desert just days after we first met, Kira dropped to the ground. I found myself dialoging with a being, an archangel, through Kira's body. "Congratulations, you have found each other again," he said, and detailed our mission together should we choose it: to deliver nine books to humanity, sharing the path of Self-Ascension©.

I was in shock. I looked deeply into Kira's eyes, which were radiating brilliant light, and felt my heart melt. I began to cry as this angelic energy spoke again. When the angel left, Kira looked at me, saw my tears and said, "What happened? I feel so filled with love and beauty!" From that moment on, we have been charged with the gift of assisting humanity. We are here to help you remember who *you* are. Now is the moment for YOUR own Sacred Reunion with the self.

Humanity has been living in a cycle of mind chatter. We analyze, scrutinize, mechanize; we do our best to complicate just about everything. However, a new way of navigating is at hand: you will simply not be able to think your way through the coming years, and especially the rapidly escalating energy of 2012. You are being called to a new life, a life that is far beyond any mentalized form.

> *Now is the moment for YOUR own*
> *Sacred Reunion with the self.*

Many writings on 2012 provide well-rationalized proposals, answers, pictures and, of course, predictions. These types of approaches, or seeking someone else's solutions from the outer world, will not open the mystical gateway of carrying you to *your* highest potential. Your purpose is to walk within a place of trust on the Earth, rather than give up your power to someone who has a perceived credential. Once we break free of the illusion, we discover that we only need credentials when it comes to inventing machines within the mandates of our societal structures. Your highest degree, you best credential, is *your life*! You are an integral part of this amazing organism that is humanity.

The blessing of the speeding up of time, the way we are navigating the planet and the way we are co-creating is that *everything* is designed to assist you to remember the truth of who you are while you still have a body. This is the essence of Self-Ascension and the opportunity of 2012: to empower this gift. This is the powerful moment, the rare and glorious opportunity for extraordinary spiritual expansion. Yet some feel that the change in the air, and the future of our world, is out of their hands. The truth is, we are *all* still collectively writing the book on 2012, and beyond. Every one of us is a co-author, and we will be finishing that book together right up until the moment of divine convergence, when the cycles begin again.

KIRA'S VISION OF 2012

I was born clairvoyant. When I was five years old, I had a profound vision of 2012. It was a humid summer day, and I was standing at the screen door staring at my mother's big, beautiful rose bushes when the world suddenly appeared black and white. I was paralyzed with fear, unable to scream, and then I heard a horrible noise—even as an adult it scares me to discuss it. The sound, like the loudest thunder you've ever heard, was in me. Not around me, *in me*. I couldn't escape it.

My eyes drawn to the horizon, I saw a big bubble coming up from the ground, like a mushroom cloud, and as it lifted everything got darker and louder. Another bubble came up, then another, until there were four. I was shaking, and out of nowhere I said, "God, I can't do this. I made a mistake. Take me before this ever happens." Keep in mind I had no experience of religion; we didn't talk about religion in my family. There was no reason for me to call out to God. Still, I received an answer.

The most beautiful voice I've ever heard grabbed me; it was like being hugged by God. The voice said, "YOU will not be here. This is only one potential for this world, and the year is 2012." Again, I was only five, and had no concept of 2012, no knowledge of the Maya, and no relationship with angels or God. Still, I knew in that moment that I was making an agreement with the divine. And, I now know that we as humanity do not have to manifest the end result I saw. *This vision is but one choice for this world*. With every choice we make and every breath we take, we must remember what a gift they are.

Half of my vision has already come true. The five-year-old girl will not be here for 2012, because I died of cancer on the operating table in 1989. I am now on this planet by conscious choice; I chose to be here during this extraordinary time. You have your own choices to make, and *your decisions* will impact the future of humanity. It is only your doubt that would stop your greatest freedom from unfolding.

THE PEOPLE OF HONEY

A few years after we were reunited in the desert, we were guided to Guatemala, to forge deep and personal partnerships with the Mayan elders of the highlands. One of the many things we delight in is that, when we visit with indigenous people, their simple wisdom evokes deep spiritual reflection and revelation.

> *When the Maya say we are becoming the people of honey, the larger context is that we are returning to a state of exquisite balance and harmony for all of humanity: The time of honey IS the golden age.*

Deep within the highland rainforests, the Maya have the sweetest little bees, not much bigger than the very tip of your smallest finger. They do not even have stingers. Beautiful winged creatures, they are in harmony with the orchids, cultivating nectar and producing honey for the community. The Maya know that because the bees are in a delicate balance with nature, they can only harvest one tablespoon of honey per year. That honey becomes very precious medicine and is never abused.

The Maya tell us we are ending the time of the people of maize (corn), and becoming the people of honey. People of maize need to take from the Earth. They need to dig in their heels and plant something, forcing it to grow. They worry about whether the rain will come, if insects will infect the crops, if the harvest will yield enough. From this place of fear and lack, the people of maize end up stealing, begging or blaming.

When the Maya say we are becoming the people of honey, the larger context is that we are returning to a state of exquisite balance and harmony for all of humanity: The time of honey IS the golden age. It is a level of harmony we have not yet enjoyed, because of the ego imbalance present inherent within the maize people. Honey is a gift that is cultivated through patience, flowers and love. When we allow ourselves to embrace our authentic selves, to welcome each other as the people of honey, we let go of the concepts of fear, lack and blame. Together, we enter a time of acceptance and bounty.

SELF-ASCENSION

The Archangel Zadkiel laughs when we speak of Self-Ascension. "What is all of this talk about ascension? How can you ascend back to what you already are? There is one self, your authentic self, who you are. You do not have a separate, higher self." The ego self—personality *and* ego—is a refraction of the true self, like a crystal in the window; you see the colors instead of the entire crystal. That

> *Self-Ascension is in service to the soul, and in service to humanity. It is a welcoming of the time of honey. And you will not ascend until you are ready to remember who you are while you have a body.*

refracted self—the maize self—is the one people have identified with for so long. They have lost sight of the fact that their truth is the God-self, the brilliant crystal. Self-Ascension is in service to the soul, and in service to humanity. It is a welcoming of the time of honey. And you will not ascend until you are ready to remember who you are while you have a body.

There is a tribe in Africa that encircles and loves wrongdoers until they remember who they are. Fellow tribespeople rehabilitate each other through the gift of divine remembrance: "You are loved, and loving, and your actions are a sign that you forgot who you are." We are at the moment in time where each one of us gets to have clear vision again—if we choose to do so. When you allow yourself to pay attention to everything that the universe is conspiring to help you with, you release thinking and start accepting your truth once again. 2010 initiates the time of the Great Acceptance, and is the beginning of the larger release of fear and doubt. It is the beginning of remembering who you are, encircling yourself and others in the heart-centered actions of true love!

The mind can rationalize any situation, such as, "Killing is wrong, but we'll execute you if you do it." Yet the heart is always moral; it cannot make this rationalization. Ultimately, it is in our hearts that we once again will reclaim the truth of who we are in a moment of pure, clear breath, free from the constriction of mind. There *will* be a 2013. Will you choose to focus on the darker vision, the cloud? Or will you usher in the time of the honey people? Will you choose to remember who you are?

Sri Ram Kaa and Kira Raa are acclaimed visionaries at the forefront of the higher-consciousness movement. Newsweek *has credited Sri and Kira with "Offering global reassurance and uplifting the consciousness of the world." They are the authors of four books (three on 2012). Look for their newest book:* 2013: Mayan Sunrise *(Ulysses Press). Join them each week on their top-rated radio show,* 2012: Higher Love. *Visit their free online magazine, www.SriandKira.com, to join the show, comment and stay current on all 2012 issues. Sri and Kira founded the Avesa Quantum Healing Institute and the TOSA Center for Enlightened Living in New Mexico, USA and the TOSA La Laguna Self-Ascension Center at Lake Atitlan, Guatemala. Learn more at www.SelfAscension. com.*

Jack Allis

CONNECTING WITH THE DIVINE SPIRIT

In these times of monumental Earth changes and paradigm shifts, connecting to the divine spirit of a living universe with our vibration is the primary source of our protection, and the primary source of our power to create the new world of light and spirit. With a topic as vast and potentially complex as 2012 and the great shift, it is vitally important to keep things as simple and uncomplicated as possible. This is the essence of all true spirituality anyway—simplicity—so simple that little children understand it without even trying.

It is also the essence of virtually all the ancient prophecies, dating back tens of thousands of years and sometimes far longer, from indigenous cultures spanning the globe. This includes the Egyptians, the Maya, the Inca, numerous tribes in South America and Africa, the Hopi and virtually every other Native American tribe. These sources are far more trustworthy than mainstream, "civilized" sources, because they have retained their connection with the one true source of higher consciousness and spiritual knowledge. And that is their intimate relationship and love affair with the natural world.

The old paradigm is unsustainable—and it is collapsing, as it must, because a relationship with the natural world is precisely the connection that the Western, civilized world has lost. It has lost its connection with life's vital energy, and with the rhythm and flow of life, and fallen into the fatal trap of placing its primary emphasis on the material world at the expense of the spiritual.

Ancient indigenous cultures, at least the ones that weren't contaminated or totally destroyed by Western civilization, never lost their intimate connection with the natural world. Their keen observations of natural cycles allowed them to become expert astronomers, scientists and cosmologists, as well as sorcerers and magicians who were capable of stupendous feats that apparently violated the rules of ordinary, linear, cause-and-effect reality.

> *The old paradigm is unsustainable—and it is collapsing, as it must, because a relationship with the natural world is precisely the connection that the Western, civilized world has lost.*

And as far as *the shift* is concerned, and this extraordinary time we are now living in, these prophecies all had the same basic message for us. This time completes a twenty-six-thousand-year galactic cycle, in which the old world, one of materiality and the attempt to control the forces of nature, will collapse. There will be an opportunity to create an entirely new world, one that is governed by the spirit. Winter Solstice 2012 is the date most prophecies point to, and these changes are predicted to occur in the window of time around it (though we have no way of precisely knowing how large the window is).

However, this is not going to just happen by itself. It's up to the human beings of the planet Earth to make it happen. And there's only one way to do this, and that is with the power of our higher consciousness and spirituality. This process of potential transformation is one of ascension—ascension from heavy to light, from higher density to lower density, and from lower frequency to higher frequency. And these Earth changes and this "shift" will be a monumental challenge for the inhabitants of the planet.

This has happened before; the changes were colossal in nature and probably will be again. The possibilities include the reversal of the Earth's magnetic poles and its rotation, great floods, intense winds, greatly increased earthquake and volcano activity as well as the disappearance of some land masses and emergence of others—the equivalent of a massive face-lift or cleansing.

The prophecies also agree that those human beings who are not prepared, and who don't have their act together energetically and spiritually, could be in for a very rough ride, possibly ending in the extinction of the entire species. But again, it's up to us.

The fate of the planet rests in our hands, and it is clear what we are called upon to do. To call this story the most important of our time is a silly understatement. Simplicity here, again, is so vitally important because few topics have been as needlessly complicated and confused as *the shift*—invariably resulting in the stimulation of hysterical fear and catastrophic visions of doomsday scenarios, which was not the intent of the prophecies.

> *The fate of the planet rests in our hands, and it is clear what we are called upon to do.*

As glorious as the Internet revolution has been in giving masses of people exposure to a vast frontier of unfiltered information, it also has its flipside. Sometimes too much can simply be too much, when any zealot or nutcase has equal access to this medium and can use it to get their message out there. The same principle applies to what are known as "disinformants." There are those among us, usually in positions of power, whose true agenda is not the spiritual fulfillment and liberation of the human race, but rather its suppression and enslavement. I refer to them as *the dark side*.

The Internet is a perfect medium for *the dark side* to disseminate false information (misinformation, propaganda, brainwashing), the purpose of which is to confuse the issues and knock people off the track of truth, with the objective of enhancing *the dark side's* power over them. Not everybody is who they say they are, and disinformants are rampant throughout our world. Sadly, this is painfully true in such ostensibly benevolent settings as the New Age movement and the green movement.

This energetic view of the world was confirmed by quantum science, which discovered a world where everything, in its essence, is interconnected energy—energy which is governed by an unseen intelligence of some kind. This, of course, is the essence of true spirituality.

All of which means it is incumbent on each of us to be aware of this, to filter through the vast sea of information with due diligence, and to decide what is right and wrong for us. Things are never as complicated—or as terrifying—as they are usually made out to be. A good standard rule is: if it's too complicated, or if it doesn't feel good, look somewhere else.

Connecting with the divine spirit of a living universe with our vibration—this is the primary source of our protection and our power. It sounds nice and sweet and simple to me, but it might sound vague or esoteric to others. It really isn't. We are not just our physical bodies. We are our totality—body, mind and spirit. As Don Juan, the Mexican Indian sorcerer from the writings of Carlos Castaneda, says: we are luminous beings. In altered states of consciousness, the sorcerers of Don Juan's lineage saw humans as egg-shaped clusters of luminous fibers that possess awareness and are connected to all the energy that surrounds them in the entire universe. These infinite connections form something like a gigantic spider's web of luminosity.

This energetic view of the world was confirmed by quantum science, which discovered a world where everything, in its essence, is interconnected energy—energy which is governed by an unseen intelligence of some kind. This, of course, is the essence of true spirituality. Like all energy, we have a vibration, a frequency. And there is a direct relationship between our energetic vibration and our emotions and thoughts. Emotions and thoughts are, actually, energy flowing through the pathways of our physical body and beyond.

There is unanimous agreement among all spiritual traditions worth their salt, from everywhere on the planet—past and present—that human beings are at their spiritual peak when they experience life with certain feelings and thoughts. Specifically, these feelings are feelings of relaxation, peacefulness, joy and love. And these thoughts spring from a mind that is quiet and still, that sees the brilliance of the world. When we experience life in this peak spiritual state, it puts us in alignment or resonance with all the other energetic and spiritual forces in our world and in the universe at large. This is what it means to be in the rhythm and flow of life. This is when our spiritual power is at its maximum. And this vibrational connection is the one true source of manifesting what we want in life. Everything, ultimately, springs from our connection with spirit.

> *And this vibrational connection is the one true source of manifesting what we want in life. Everything, ultimately, springs from our connection with spirit.*

In order to create the new world, we must make this energetic and spiritual connection both as individuals and in *critical mass*. *Critical mass* is the energetic point at which a sufficient number of human beings have retained this connection, and when amazing and unprecedented things will start to happen. Like the hundredth-monkey effect, once enough of us reconnect with our spiritual power, we become a force that cannot be stopped—and we won't need crumbling political, economic, religious and social structures to help. No thank you—we can handle it on our own.

As David Rhodes, one of the heroes of my novel, *Infinity's Flower,* says: "If we are in tune with the Earth, and if we are in tune with the divine spirit, then the Earth and the divine spirit will shower us with unimaginable blessings." This is the source of our protection and power in the face of this challenge or any other, and that's all we need.

Jack Allis is the author of the blockbuster novel Infinity's Flower—A Tale of 2012 & the Great Shift of the Ages. *Since its publication in September 2007, Jack has become the living embodiment of its message, traveling the country and delivering the message to as many awakening souls as he can reach through sacred chants, his groundbreaking PowerPoint presentation, 2012 & the Shift— Transforming Challenges into Blessings (soon to be released as a book) and an ever-expanding number of TV and radio interviews. He is the author of two other novels,* Infinity's Children *and* Masters of Destiny, *as well as his popular monthly e-newsletter.*

Jack practices what he preaches, living minimally and close to nature in a tiny cottage on Little Okauchee Lake in Wisconsin. He is also a personal growth and spiritual teacher. In his teaching work (in person or via telephone or Internet), Jack shows people how to connect with the divine spirit of a living universe using the power of their vibration, and how to manifest their dreams by living life with feelings of peacefulness, joy, love and acceptance. To learn more about Jack, visit www.JackAllis.com.

Aurora Juliana Ariel, PhD

EARTH 2012:
THE VIOLET PEOPLE

Forever, the world has held universal mythologies around the idea that Earth was once an Eden—and that we have been cast out, and must toil and suffer. And yet people have always longed for peace on Earth. So far, this longing has eluded humanity in every century. The reason for this lies in the subconscious patterns that hold us victim to our unconscious selves and keep us disempowered. I found a way out, a way to restore inner peace quickly and to fulfill our highest destiny potential, rather than accepting the fate dictated by our patterns. There is a cure. And it can come only from within.

I have dedicated many years to pioneering work in the psyche; I found the cause of suffering, and developed a cure in TheQuest™. I have also tracked and encountered the presence of millions of extraordinary, visionary members of the human race that I call the Violet People. Thanks in great part to my awareness of this new Violet Tribe, I have developed a deep and abiding belief that, though the prophecies surrounding our time portend great suffering for humanity, we have the power to create an alternative future—a realized vision of peace, harmony, love, joy and health for the entire planet. And the Violet People are here to show us the way to that glorious future.

Most people on the planet today believe that their dramas, hardships, illnesses and negative relationship dynamics are the product of something outside themselves. They think their problems are unfixable. But what I've found, in many years as a research psychologist and healer, is that these issues are caused by subconscious patterns born of misconceptions about ourselves; the belief systems we develop over time, and especially in early childhood. Those subconscious patterns can be recognized and altered, paving the way for others and creating a new paradigm, a ripple effect of consciousness and peace.

> *There is a cure. And it can come only from within.*

At this time in history, we're being called to a new frontier. We've become technologically advanced, but our consciousness has not advanced along with technology. That is why we are facing particularly painful times. My faith in the human potential to heal our long legacy of unconsciousness has led me to develop a breakthrough self-healing system called TheQuest, which offers tools for accelerated understanding of both our shadow sides and our authentic selves and expression of that authentic self in every person. I am so committed to helping people in this important time that I am giving my new book, *TheQuest: Heal Your Life, Change Your Destiny* for FREE, forever, as my sacred offering to a world in transition. TheQuest can heal this legacy of suffering and actualize Eden by moving humanity forward into a way of harmony and peace that is a reflection of our authentic selves.

The Violet People began to arrive on Earth fairly recently. Before their arrival, ideals of unity, harmony and peace were sentiments mostly left to religious manuscripts and a few sages and teachers such as Buddha and Jesus who appeared in each age. For the most part, humanity has remained separatist, jealously guarding individual beliefs or cultures as removed from universal law and, almost always, as the "only way." Peace, love, tolerance and harmony have not been hallmarks of human history—so far. That is why the Violet People are here, to lead us into a more enlightened future.

Though threads of their visionary approach to life on Earth have appeared throughout the ages, the real impact of the Violet People was not felt until the 1960s, when a whole host of movements—the peace movement, the civil rights movement, the environmental movement and the human potential movement—emerged. Since that time, because of the presence of the Violet People, the world has begun a tremendous shift in consciousness as light begins to break through the darkness, and clear vision and powerful intention replace apathy.

We've all heard the dark prophecies around 2012, but many also prophesy joyously of the arrival of a tribe destined to take the planet through profound change. Some of the most powerful prophecies come from the Indian Nations. Lee Standing Bear Moore of the Manataka American Indian Council said, "They will bring balance and harmony back to Mother Earth ... They will be pathfinders leading the way to a new universe, a new reality ... bringing together the four races of man to live in peace. The four sacred directions and the four races of man are symbolized by the magnificence and glory of the rainbow. The people of the Rainbow will give praise for the blessings of the Creator's loving grace."

> *Our ultimate quest as human beings is to alter our subconscious patterns, and heal the unconsciousness that causes our suffering—and the world's—by delving deeply for inner truth and transformation.*

I have long tracked and studied these "Rainbow" Violets, and I estimate that between 80 million and 100 million of them are now here on the planet. These spiritual seekers—these visionary creators—move on an inner quest for truth, inspiring everyone around them.

They are born to fulfill an extraordinary destiny and heed their inner calling to heal and transform our planet in an unprecedented shift from the unconscious to a conscious collective path.

Though Violet People have been and are being born into every culture and nation, they share a signature set of attributes, which I call Master Qualities. I have listed these twenty-two Master Qualities in my second book of the Earth 2012 series, *Earth 2012: Time of the Awakening Soul, How Millions of People Are Changing Our Future.* You can take the test and see whether you are a Violet Person.

The Violet People tend to follow the beat of their own drums rather than the status quo. Violets are highly sensitive and need to renew themselves in solitude and nature. They seek altered states such as meditation and prayer, and are highly creative free spirits, conscious individuals (in the true sense of the word) who thrive on self-discovery and the quest for truth. Violet People cannot abide the cultural amnesia of unconsciousness. In their quest for truth and service to humanity, they delve deeply into themselves to find the source of their subconscious patterning and wrestle with it earnestly, sometimes with great pain. Thus they learn from life's challenges, continually strive for self-improvement and seek to find and fulfill their unique purpose. Loving parents and wise children, they are open and communicative, thriving on authenticity and direct, vivid life experience. Ever on a spiritual quest, they are mystics, visionaries, humanitarians, environmentalists and universal thinkers deeply in touch with the concept of unity.

Encoded in the heart of the Violet Race is the utopian Ideal, the Eden we all long for and which the Violet People believe is being reborn. They inspire others, through their own vision and hard work, to high ideals and noble endeavors, paving the way for millions of souls who, on fire with a sacred vision, can rise to play their roles in birthing this new Eden. It is no accident that the Violet People are here to help the Earth at the eleventh hour. This great influx of mysticism is unparalleled in Earth's history, and is a call to all of us to make an extraordinary effort during this transition. The Violet People are here to show us our great potential and lead the way to our glorious future. The planet direly needs our collective assistance if we are to pass through this era's gateway and fulfill our destiny as a loving, harmonious people—friends to our fellow creatures and caring stewards of our environment.

You may recognize yourself as a Violet person. Wonderful! Whether you are or not, your presence on Earth is now significant. And, you are surrounded by Violet People who can help inspire your own spiritual development and advancement. They are everywhere, and are uncannily able to find each other, gathering to spearhead beautiful projects and collectives. They even have their own consciousness language. I have recognized Violet People in my own family, and many Violet children are being born across the Earth with distinctive Indigo, Crystal, Dolphin, or Rainbow qualities.

> *The planet direly needs our collective assistance if we are to pass through this era's gateway and fulfill our destiny as a loving, harmonious people—friends to our fellow creatures and caring stewards of our environment.*

Whether you believe you are a Violet Person or not, you have great gifts and talents to lend to the present planetary equation, and you *can* make a difference. Cultivate the qualities of the Violet People to discover your authentic self. The planet needs *you*.

Remember, there is no outward force at work punishing you. If you feel oppressed, your oppressor is your unconscious patterns, and you have the power to change this. We must now take responsibility for ourselves and for our own healing, embarking on the ultimate quest so we can lend our fire to the great vision being birthed for our New Eden, our New World.

Aurora Juliana Ariel, PhD, creator of TheQuest™ and award-winning author of the Earth 2012 *series, is a pioneering doctor, healer, and teacher whose research and work have given her a profound understanding of the psyche and the tools to heal an ailing humanity. Dr. Ariel trained under pioneering doctors in alternative medicine, psychology and holistic health, and holds over thirty-five certificates and degrees in advanced healing methods as well as a BA, MA and PhD in psychology. As successor to Hawaiian Kahuna and Shaolin Grandmaster Pang, she has also been given the title of Kahuna.*

All of this pales, however, in comparison with the work Dr. Ariel has done on herself, and directly in the psyche, with countless clients over many years. That work has brought forth her landmark discoveries and the development of her counseling theory and healing practice, TheQuest. Dr. Ariel offers TheQuest as a complete self-healing system that includes a powerful "Life Mastery Path" and self-counseling technique. Her reason for offering it to the people, rather than only to professional counselors, is simple: she wants to bring healing to a world in desperate need. Her ebook, TheQuest: Heal Your Life, Change Your Destiny, *is available FREE on her website. You can download the ebook, learn about sponsorship and find more about Dr. Ariel at www.AuroraJulianaAriel.com*

Nassim Haramein

FUNDAMENTAL SCIENCE, FUNDAMENTAL CHANGE

Changes in science are underway that affect our understanding of ourselves as an integral part of a self-organizing universe, and as conscious beings that are fundamentally connected and at one with the cosmos. At the same time, new scientific theories are leading to new inventions that can bring about a society of abundance, fully free to explore this universe of which it is a part. We are witnessing changes in many different areas—in human consciousness, in our way of relating with each other, and in ecological changes within our environment that cause us, *force us*, to move forward. And the new scientific discoveries, and consequent technologies now emerging, will give us the *means* to move forward. These changes in science are leading to holistic new *types* of sciences based on more universal principles.

Some of the most fundamental beliefs we have in physics are changing. New work, new theories, are gaining momentum. For instance, my paper on the Schwarzschild proton, which describes the atomic nucleus as a miniature black hole, just won an award. The award came as a surprise, because my ideas are so radical; it demonstrates a new willingness to consider completely new theories. We're starting to realize that the structure of space-time, the dynamics of the structure of space, has a fundamental impact on our lives and on the way things work. We're not isolated; we're connected through an unseen and, until now, unmeasured energy—the energy of the vacuum.

The 2012 nexus predicts a fundamental change at all levels of human society and human consciousness. This deep change is driven by events occurring in our solar system and our galactic disc, events that were predicted by the ancient Mayan calendars. The Long Count Calendar defines the moment in history when humans are going to ascend.

> *We're not isolated; we're connected through an unseen and, until now, unmeasured energy—the energy of the vacuum.*

I believe that ascension is not just a metaphor for the evolution of consciousness, but actually has literal meaning. We will understand the principles of creation. We will understand the fundamental structure of the vacuum, the fundamental energy that connects us all. We will have advanced technology. And, we will finally learn to deal with gravity, so that we can literally lift ourselves off the planet. Gravitational drives are right around the corner. Technologies that deliver clean, continuous energy directly from the vacuum are on their way. Inventors are coming forward now with ways to draw on that energy.

Our society is a society of scarcity. We think that there is a limited amount of goods, and a limited amount of energy, and that we must fight for them. The technological changes I foresee will bring about a society grounded in the realization that we live in an incredibly energetic universe, a universe in which each atom continuously spins because of its relationship to the vacuum, and that this relationship is an unbounded source of energy. We can become self-sufficient and actually thrive, transforming into a society that truly understands there exists an infinite amount of goods, an infinite abundance, an infinite amount of energy and no need to fight for any of it.

In physics, a unified field theory is a way to express in one set of equations what we know about the electromagnetic field and the gravitational field, which we know in the big relativistic world where we live, as well as the strong and weak nuclear forces, which operate in the very small quantum world of the atom. Einstein spent most of his life working on this problem. He didn't believe in quantum theory. He thought there was a way to use his relativity equations to describe the quantum world. It's clear in our universe that the big stuff is made of the small stuff, so there shouldn't be two sets of equations in physics to describe the whole thing.

> *We can become self-sufficient and actually thrive, transforming into a society that truly understands there exists an infinite amount of goods, an infinite abundance, an infinite amount of energy and no need to fight for any of it.*

My paper on the Schwarzschild proton treats protons in the nuclei of atoms as miniature black holes, bound together by gravity. It shows that both the strong and weak nuclear forces can be described by the same equations that describe gravity and the electromagnetic forces: it is a unified field theory. A unified field theory does solve this problem in physics. But on a larger level, it includes the unification of all things; it explains the complexity of the biological world, of the chemical world, the development of consciousness, the connectedness of all things in the universe.

We are approaching a moment of discovery that will show us we are not alone, but that we are connected to all things; that every atom, every system, is actually drawing from a collective force that drives creation into existence; and that that force is in the space all around us. Because we experience space as empty, we think there is nothing there, and that everything is separate. But when we look carefully at the space between things, we find that it's not empty at all. It's absolutely full.

If you don't have a radio, or don't turn it on, you don't notice that there are radio waves around you and moving through you. But the radio waves are always there. In the same way, there is energy in the space all around you. Space, the vacuum, is very dynamic, very active and very full—when a society makes that realization, it changes fundamentally.

We are on the brink of making that realization. It's happening on many different levels, and you can see the fundamental connectivity of things emerging relentlessly in all our dealings. In ecology, we are beginning to realize that we can't just keep on cutting trees and polluting without it having an effect on other things that will affect still *other* things. The whole system is connected, interwoven in a very complex and advanced way. If we do not align our actions with this fundamental framework of nature, we will cut the branch we're sitting on. That realization is finally occurring. It's a very exciting—and challenging—moment.

> *But when we look carefully at the space between things, we find that it's not empty at all. It's absolutely full.*

I'm proposing a self-organizing mechanism, like Darwinian evolution, but at the level of fundamental physics. Because systems are connected, the vacuum is aware of everything that occurs. The atomic level feeds information to the vacuum, and the vacuum feeds energy or information back to the system. This feedback loop of information allows for evolution as systems tend to move toward higher levels of organization in order to accommodate the local environment. Our universe is a self-learning system in which the human being is one extension of space-time looking back at itself and learning.

From this theory of physics you can start to synthesize, to understand the fundamental mechanics of consciousness—not just the physics of the material world, but how consciousness emerges from it as a result of feedback dynamics in the structure of space-time, which is a feedback loop between the gravitational field and the electromagnetic field, which are the only two forces that remain after unification.

This feedback occurring everywhere is driving the whole system in a cycle that has no beginning or end. The system continually learns about itself, and as it does it creates more and more complexity, creates more and more adaptation to local environments, and it learns more and more. Every electron moves constantly through singularity and back out, through the vacuum and back out. Each time, it informs the vacuum and the vacuum informs it. All things are known by the vacuum—the total connective metric—through this feedback loop.

So we're in it. The transformation of 2012 is happening right now. Getting everybody involved in the transformation is crucial. People can move the change forward, making it smoother and easier.

I urge you to spend some time in contemplation, realizing your infinite nature, realizing your connectivity to the structure of space, to the vacuum as a whole; realizing your connectivity to all things through the inner self. All the masters who have walked the Earth have encouraged us to learn to turn our senses inward because within the atomic level, within the singularity that centers our existence is the infinite potential of creation. This is what connects us to all things.

I believe that spending more time turning your senses inward and connecting with your fundamental nature, and then applying that to the external world in your day-to-day life might be one of the most crucial, the most important, things you can do. When you align with your fundamental nature, with your singularity, with the infinite potential inside yourself, you are fundamentally aligned with your *dharma*, your mission, your deepest possible recognition of self. Such an exploration can lead to great things in your life.

Every atom of your body is connected to every other atom in the universe, as it exchanges energy and information with the vacuum. This infinite energy and knowledge can infuse your consciousness, and change your life beginning today. Do not be apprehensive about the changes clustering around 2012, for they will force us to make the evolutionary leap into a world of abundance and wonder.

———————————

Nassim Haramein has proposed a unified field theory based on a new solution to Einstein's equations. This groundbreaking theory has been delivered to the scientific community through peer-reviewed papers and presentations at international physics conferences. His research into a variety of fields, including theoretical physics, cosmology, quantum mechanics, biology, chemistry and ancient civilizations, has led to a coherent understanding of the fundamental structure of the universe. This new view leads to an in-depth change in our current perception of physics and consciousness.

Weaving together the sciences of advanced physics, cosmology, chemistry and biology as well as the wisdom of the ancients, Nassim has created an exciting tapestry of space-time that may prove to be one of the most important scientific, philosophical and technological discoveries of our time.

Nassim is Director of Research at The Resonance Project, a 501(c)(3) public charity dedicated to the exploration of unification principles and their implications in our world today. The foundation is actively developing a research park where science, sustainability, green technology and permaculture come together. Learn more about Nassim's work at www.TheResonanceProject.org.

Bob Frissell

THE SHIFT OF THE AGES

For thirteen thousand years, we have been in separation. We see everything as polarized—good or bad, up or down, hot or cold. We judge everything that happens, which keeps us in this mode of perceiving. As an example of this separate way of looking at life, if your body gets cold you think of a fire or a heater; you think of something outside yourself. This has led to our increasing dependence on technology. We become weaker when we keep giving away our power to technology—that is, to external objects. We then become dependent upon these objects, and soon get to the point where we can't do anything for ourselves.

Oneness does not understand this. It doesn't know what "needing" anything means. Aboriginals, who remain in unity-consciousness, and other indigenous people, do not know what "need" means; whatever they need just appears because they are in harmony with nature. If we really knew, we could just think the thought "warm" and it would be so. We have the capability to change anything in the reality from within. But many of us feel that we are just people, with no power and no say regarding how things are in creation. The larger truth is that we can change anything in our environment under certain circumstances—when we are in unity and not in separation. The spirit of God can move right through you.

Sixteen thousand years ago, while on Atlantis, we violated galactic law. After a disagreement about how to handle an approaching comet—the remnants of which are scattered throughout four states—the descendants of Martians decided to separate from the Atlantians. They created a powerful energy field that went totally out of control and nearly destroyed the Earth. We were on a very

> The larger truth is that we can change anything
> in our environment under certain circumstances—
> when we are in unity and not in separation.
> The spirit of God can move right through you.

high level of awareness at the time, far beyond where we are now, but by committing this illegal act we fell many dimensional levels until we landed in this current, dense aspect of the reality. There are no accidents, however. In the cosmic scheme of things, this "fall" was necessary in order to allow for a greater possibility. We are now about to leave this place of separation and return to unity-consciousness. The whole world is. We have only a short time left before we will no longer be in separation. This is not going to be happening someday; it is happening now.

DIMENSIONS

All dimensional levels of this world are here and present, right now, and interlinked. The only difference between dimensional worlds is their wavelengths. Wavelength is the key to the entire universe. Dimensions are separated from one another by wavelength in exactly the same way as notes are on a musical scale. Any octave on the piano has eight white keys and five black keys, which together give its player the chromatic scale. The thirteenth note is actually the first note of the next octave, and these octaves keep repeating themselves in either direction. Between each note and the next are twelve harmonic, holographic points; in dimensional terms these are called "overtones." That makes one hundred and forty-four dimensions in the octave.

There is a void between dimensions. Each dimension is also separated from the others by a ninety-degree rotation. If you could change wavelengths and rotate ninety degrees, you would disappear from this world and reappear in whatever dimension you were tuned to. This planet has many different worlds; they are all right here, but our consciousness is tuned to one particular wavelength. For example, if we were to go up one level, which we are in the process of doing, we would find that whatever we think, as soon as we think it, instantly manifests. We would also be in light bodies.

THE PRECESSION OF THE EQUINOXES

Earth's spin axis, in addition to being tilted twenty-three and a half degrees, wobbles. This change in position causes the equinoctial points to regress by one degree every seventy-two years; it changes the viewpoint of one zodiacal constellation every two-thousand-one-hundred-sixty years, making one complete revolution every twenty-five-thousand-nine-hundred-twenty years.

Seen from the North Pole, the axis traces an ellipse. At perigee on this ellipse, we are closest to the center of the galaxy; at apogee, we are farthest away and moving in a counter-clockwise direction. Our consciousness is directly related to this aeonic movement. As we move toward the center of the galaxy, we wake up; as we move away from the center we fall asleep. From a tiny wobble, we literally shift dimensional levels, stepping not only into brand new worlds but also into a completely different way of interpreting the one reality. Simultaneously, great physical changes occur—no less than the poles shifting (i.e., the planet turning over in space).

It is not at the two points closest and farthest from the center of the galaxy where this shift happens, but rather at two points nine hundred years removed from each of them. We sit, now, right at the turning point of beginning to move back toward the center of the galaxy and start waking up. At one-hundred-eighty degrees opposite the last shift, the next one is imminent.

Though there has been great fear over the coming changes, with certain groups of people building shelters and storing food, fearful that land-masses will sink, that may not happen this time; it may be a more gentle ride. The speed at which we are evolving is changing everything. We are moving so quickly that a whole new possibility never before dreamed of is emerging. For a complete understanding, please see *Nothing in This Book Is True, But It's Exactly How Things Are.*

> *We sit, now, right at the turning point of beginning to move back toward the center of the galaxy and start waking up. At one-hundred-eighty degrees opposite the last shift, the next one is imminent.*

HOPI PROPHECY FULFILLED

Comet 17P/Holmes shocked astronomers on October 24, 2007, with a spectacular eruption. By mid-November the expanding comet had become the most visible object in the solar system—bigger even than the sun. Since then, the comet has faded back into invisibility.

This exploding "Blue Star" was the fulfillment of a two-hundred-year-old Hopi prophecy, opening a seven-year window and putting us in the "end times." The Maya are in agreement with the Hopi, as both cultures are conscious survivors of Atlantis and hold the memory of Earth's past twenty-six thousand years.

This means that sometime between now and 2015 or so, we are very likely to experience changes almost greater than our ability to imagine: a physical pole shift, along with a consciousness shift into the fourth dimension. The exact date, according to the Maya, will almost certainly not be December 21, 2012; rather, it will happen sometime in this seven-year window.

The Maya remember the last shift, along with the one twenty-six thousand years ago. They say there are certain internal changes we must make in order not only to survive, but also rise to the next level. The keys, they say, are to stay out of fear, to be calm and balanced and to be in the heart. They say that Mother Earth knows the vibration of the heart, and that she will protect you through these times.

KUNDALINI AND THE BIRTH OF THE UNITY GRID

Since the dawning of the new millennium, two events have occurred that are changing everything. The first is the movement of the Earth's Kundalini, which happens every thirteen thousand years and is tied to the precession of the equinoxes. The Kundalini is related to the Earth's spiritual growth process. Every time it moves, it has a new vibration, which in turn takes us to a new level of consciousness.

The second major event was the birthing of the new grid in January, 2008. A grid is a geometrical, electromagnetically shaped

> *Mother Earth has made a conscious decision to move into the higher overtones of the fourth dimension.*

"fishnet" about sixty miles above the globe, encircling the entire planet. Each of the Earth's approximately fourteen million species has its own grid; humankind has three grids, one for each level of consciousness. The conception of the new grid began thirteen-thousand-two-hundred years ago. The recent birth of the completed grid lasted about one month, with the assistance of Polynesian elders. The unity-consciousness grid has been fully formed and birthed. It is now alive and conscious; it is a living energy field around the Earth, and this changes everything. Mother Earth has made a conscious decision to move into the higher overtones of the fourth dimension.

These two events have put us into a different potential world. We are now in a heart-based energy field; when you connect to it, a new possibility opens up. This means that our spiritual acceleration will quicken dramatically—there is nothing left to stop it.

It also means that within the next seven years or so (from October 24, 2007), the entire cycle that we are in now will disappear in a single day. In its place, a whole new world will be birthed, one based not on the mind, but rather on the heart. We are right on the edge of the emergence of this world. Everything is in place; the Kundalini has moved; the grid is alive. Yet most of the world continues in its old pattern, thinking this is the way it will be forever and hardly imagining that something incredible is about to occur.

This is a time of great celebration, as we move out of the darkness and into the light. The veils will be lifted; we will remember and live our intimate connection to all life; we will be allowed to reunite with our cosmic brothers and to move about the universe. We will completely redefine what it means to be human!

Bob Frissell is a master rebirther and teacher of thirty years whose books are regarded as underground spiritual classics. In addition to Nothing in This Book Is True But It's Exactly How Things Are, *he is the author of* Something in This Book Is True *and* You Are a Spiritual Being Having a Human Experience. *His books have been published in seventeen languages and are available in more than thirty countries. Bob has been a featured speaker at The Global Congress of Spiritual Scientists in Bangalore, India, the 4th Annual Symbiosis Gathering at Yosemite, The Prophets Conference in Tulum and many New Living Expos. He has also appeared on numerous talk shows, including* The Jeff Rense Program, *and has been a three-time guest on* Coast to Coast AM. *He has presented his workshops throughout North America and Europe.*

Bob was trained by Leonard Orr, the rebirthing pioneer, and by Drunvalo Melchizedek, the originator of the Mer-Ka-Ba and Unity Breath meditations. He gives private rebirthing sessions along with his two workshops: "The Breath of Life (Rebirthing and Emotional Healing)" and "The Flower of Life (Sacred Geometry and the Mer-Ka-Ba)." Visit www.BobFrissell.com.

Dr. Melissa Andersson

ENERGY, MAGIC AND MIRACLES

My heart is pounding as if my chest will explode. A shaman is leading us deep into the Andes. I'm climbing down a remote mountain so steep that one misstep can send me plunging to the canyon floor and certain death. We are on our way to an extremely remote abandoned Inca city. I'm hours into the descent on the barren rocky terrain. I've lost my footing several times and barely escaped plummeting down the mountain. My knees, hips and ankles have strained so hard that they have nearly given out in exhaustion. I'm crawling now, clinging to the mountainside with hands that are strained and bleeding. After six hours I reach the canyon floor. Others in our group are faring worse than I am. I watch with concern as some are carried down the mountain with joint injuries and blood oozing from their hands and feet.

The travel flyer advertising this journey referred to this part of the two-week Peruvian experience with shamans as a five-day "camping trip on horseback—no experience necessary." "I can do that," I thought. "Sitting on a horse is easy." It turns out that the terrain is so steep that the little horses and donkeys can't carry the weight of humans on the descent without the risk of tumbling headfirst down the mountain.

I came to Peru in gratitude and celebration for having recently recovered from a sudden, mysterious illness.

My heart had gone into crisis and become enlarged. I had symptoms of multiple sclerosis. Many times my body became spastic and uncontrollable, and I'd find myself falling painfully to the ground. At the time, I thought lunging across a living room was hard. On these remote mountains, one uncoordinated move could send me flying thousands of feet down into an abyss of no return.

I'd been determined to uncover and address the cause of my former symptoms. For years, I'd studied natural medicine, indigenous healing, mind/body medicine, quantum methods and energy medicine. I wasn't about to give up and spend the rest of my life in a wheelchair without a leave-no-stone-unturned research mission to get to the bottom of why my body had gone into crisis. Ultimately, I discovered environmental poisoning at the core. By the time I got to Peru, I had been recovered for a few months. I knew I wasn't in marathon-running shape, but I could certainly go camping and sit on a horse.

*I came to Peru in gratitude and celebration
for having recently recovered from
a sudden, mysterious illness.*

The impetus for the trip was my desire to learn from the Andean shamans, especially the Q'ero Elders. The Q'ero are the descendants of the Inca, among those whom the conquistadors sought to massacre. Over five hundred years ago, the Q'ero retreated high into the Andes to preserve their body of knowledge and healing—and only recently began interacting with the outside world again, bringing forth their prophecies.

As a healer, I had felt extremely blessed to meet the Q'ero. The Q'ero are in conscious connection with what they call *kawsay pacha*—the cosmos of living energy. Most ancient cultures naturally tapped into energy fields for healing. I like to think of them as "ancient quantum physicians."

What a joy it was to learn from keepers of ancient wisdom who'd been uninfluenced by the modern world! Before they discussed healing on an individual basis, they wanted to talk about a much greater healing—the healing of our world. They talked about the *pachacuti*—the great shift of the ages (what we've come to refer to as 2012) and asked us to help them carry this very important message to the world. They explained that now is the time when harmony and order will be restored and the world will be turned right-side-up again. They spoke about the care and refinement of our light bodies and advised us how we can best prepare for this evolutionary shift of the Earth and human consciousness. The Q'ero talked about how, with proper energy alignment, we can evolve as new humans, which they call *homo luminous*. They gifted us with ceremonies and powerful transmissions of energy. All too soon, it was time for our tiny group to leave the Q'ero and move on. As we said goodbye, one of the Elders looked deep into my eyes, smiled and said, "Welcome home."

I'd lived life aligned with the powerful possibilities of the universe. These truths brought me to overcome a childhood of illness and perceived limitations. It was working with cancer patients and the emotional aspects of illness years ago that called me deeper on the path. To bring in more energy tools, I'd spent weeks on top of a mountain in Italy training as a certified firewalk instructor. I also brought together many heart-opening processes (which did not require fire) and created breakthrough "power programs" for cancer patients that energized joy, inner power and triumph of the human spirit. Eventually I expanded these programs to mind/body/spirit conferences and to corporations, where they have been enormously popular.

We are blessed to have many authors and scientists teaching us about quantum physics, the law of attraction, epigenetics and human/global transformation. I help people have experiences that facilitate the energetic shifts these teachers write about, and raise their vibrations to the "miracle frequencies" of love, hope, joy, laughter, inner-power, play and human/spiritual connection. We make quantum shifts in the "miracle zone."

Yet now, on the mountain expedition that followed my time with the Q'ero Elders, I feel horribly unprepared. The peace and joy I felt with the Elders in the sacred valley near Cuzco feels light years away as I look up at the next mountains in the series of mountains we are to trek. They look higher and steeper than the one we just descended.

I soon learn that no one in our group—not even the pack animal handlers—has risked this trek before. It will take us two more days to get to the sacred site, and another two and a half days to get back out again to any semblance of civilization. I am seriously concerned that we will not all get back out alive. I decide to stay alone in the canyon and rejoin the group on their return. "You'll have your guts ripped out and eaten by nightfall," our leader responds. I know he is referring to the puma (mountain lion) that has been tracking us since we began.

> *We make quantum shifts in the "miracle zone."*

Despite my concern for everyone's safety, our leader insists on pushing forward to the ruins. Between mountains and a mountain lion, I don't have much choice. I find a little horse, bless him and drag myself onto his back for the terrifying upward climb.

We navigate narrow switchback paths created by the Inca long before horses came to Peru. I can almost see the Inca climbing higher and higher tiers with strong legs, strong arms and broad chests designed for scaling this rugged, high altitude terrain. Unfortunately, the climb requires my horse to jump up in the air and flip his body to land in the opposite direction at the upper switchbacks. Doing this, his rump swings out over the cliffs with me clinging to his back. With no physical strength left to hang on, every moment that I'm not flung off the mountain seems to be a miracle. I use everything that I know about how the mind affects the body to modulate my fear and calm my heart. I maintain myself in constant prayer. I wrap a bubble of love around my horse and myself and send the loving bubble down through the mountain and back up to the heavens again. The Andeans believe that Apus, the mountains, are sacred spirits towering in the sky to act like antennas to God. I lovingly connect with the Apu and ask for protection.

> *The Andeans believe that Apus, the mountains, are sacred spirits towering in the sky to act like antennas to God. I lovingly connect with the Apu and ask for protection.*

We are less than halfway up the mountain when the sky cracks open with torrential rain. With horses slipping in the mud and sliding into each other, near-chaos ensues. I need to continue on foot. I will my legs to climb, but they appear to have the endurance of wet noodles. With each step, I use everything I have ever learned about energy, prayer and intention to find strength. We climb from the searing heat of the tropical canyon to the freezing cold of the cloud forest. By nightfall I crawl into my drenched sleeping bag, cold to the bone and extremely grateful to be alive.

We did make it to the Inca city of Choquequirao (and back out again alive). I was awed and humbled by her sacred magnificence. And when I remember the dozens of condors flying above us as if they heard our call when we offered ceremony, I still become overwhelmed with emotion. Local shamans tell me that since my time there, a less treacherous route to the site has opened up. And yet, reflective of the larger picture of life, it's not so much about reaching a destination as it is about embracing the journey. It's about what life teaches us and what we are capable of as humans when our comfort zones are pulled away from us. It is said that, energetically, the journey to 2012 can be a rocky one. We may see lots of peaks and valleys as we move towards the magnificence of the shift and beyond.

I'm thrilled to be here during this wonderful time as one of the many people helping humanity and the Earth transform through 2012. This is a time to return to simple, yet profound, wisdom, energetic connections and the healing that the ancient ones were in harmony with. It's a time to find courage and break through fears and perceived limitations. This is a time of love, heightened energy and aligning with miracles. May each of us manifest abundantly and bring peace and love to each other and the world.

––––––––––

Dr. Melissa Andersson is a positive breakthrough specialist, international speaker and transformational leader. An inspiring and powerful visionary, she has been mission-driven since childhood to uplift humanity and our magnificent planet. In 2003 she received a "Humanitarian of the Year" award for her volunteer work around the world. Drawing from a background as a Doctor of Natural Medicine (and how the mind affects the body) with certifications in pastoral counseling, mental health field traumatology, hypnotherapy and firewalk instruction and specialties in kinesiology, stress relief and energy psychology, her methods bring results.

Dr. Melissa's passion is to bring more joy, healing and abundance to the world. She does this through speaking and facilitating at conferences and through her "Awaken Your Inner Awesome®: Breakthrough to Abundance" seminars and retreats. Dr. Melissa is the bestselling co-author of The Law of Business Attraction: Secrets to Cooperative Success. *She has created self-help CDs and videos, and a forthcoming book and workbook on breakthroughs. As an event host/ emcee, she has a phenomenal ability to open hearts and energize joy, excitement and human connection. Learn more about Dr. Melissa at www.HumanPotentialCentral.com and www.TransformationalTravels. com.*

Amirah Hall

PARTICIPATION IS VITAL

In the years surrounding 2012, we are taking a quantum leap in consciousness. Human evolution will change reality as we know it. Living at the end of an era and beginning an entirely different one, we possess identities that are shape-shifting right along with the dimensional shift 2012 signifies. This creates a tremendous opportunity for us to learn about and participate in our own great spiritual awakening and expansion.

In 1998, I had a near-death experience. I learned that we are each one with all of creation and that the fabric of creation is love. I received firsthand knowledge that we are light beings, born as pure light into a human body. As we grow, our memory of our true nature and the source from which we came begins to fade. Our divine light dims as we struggle to survive in our human body. Our purpose is to reclaim and reignite that light. It's a process of reawakening and remembering.

We are stepping into a new form of reality, away from the ignorance and amnesia we've experienced for millennia and back into that divine light. We have agreed to incarnate here and now to participate in this new reality. So it is imperative that we prepare by releasing fear and limiting beliefs. Then, as we come to understand and remember our true nature, we can fully experience the genius of our species. It's ready and available for all of us to harvest. As we rediscover our spiritual abilities, we awaken to our full potenial.

Since my life-changing experience over ten years ago, I have been preparing, growing and healing. I didn't know, then, what I was preparing for. Over time, I began to realize that I am here to help lead others to increased awareness. I'm here to share my message and mentor others who seek validation and encouragement during this time of awakening.

> *Our purpose is to reclaim and reignite that light.*
> *It's a process of reawakening and remembering.*

On December 21, 2012, our Earth and sun will be in precise alignment with the center of our galaxy. We are already feeling the momentum of the shift as we approach this pinnacle point. And as we build to it, we feel an acceleration of huge change building on every level. Our physical bodies are changing. Our consciousness—that part of us that is not visible—is changing, too. We have an incredible opportunity to be fully aware and awake when this galactic alignment occurs.

As physical beings, connected to the Earth and the galaxy, we experience the same electromagnetic and energetic changes that are taking place on our planet and beyond. Many are experiencing physical symptoms resulting from Earth changes already. They may have joint pain, foggy thinking, feelings of disorientation and anxiety. Why? They are receiving physical messages that they can't continue to conduct their lives in the same way. They might quit their jobs, sell all their possessions and move halfway around the world.

The changes we're experiencing are not just physical. We are being energetically re-patterned. The status quo will no longer do. Our old way of being is in a state of deconstruction. How we think and act, our competitiveness, aggression and focus on material gain, are all being torn apart. More and more frequently, we are seeing beyond the veil of the third dimension and encountering nonphysical beings, hearing voices we don't recognize. We are increasingly sensitized to others' thoughts and subtle shifts of energy within and without us.

All these changes might feel scary. There's an energetic quickening occurring; pressure unrelated to the stresses of jobs, finances and families is building. People are wondering, "What is going *on?*" Well—it's the end of life as we've known it. No old formulas or solutions will work in the beginning of this new era. Our challenge is to cultivate a new vision of relationship to self and others so we can reconnect with our light. Learning practical steps will facilitate and support us as we transition from closing times into opening times.

We have the power to direct our paths along the lines we choose. We're moving into a place where multiple dimensions intersect. If we're game, if we're up for it, it will be a party. What we need to realize is that we *have* the tools to meet ourselves in higher consciousness. Guidance is available to us from within, from teachers on Earth and from teachers beyond this dimension. All we have to do is choose to listen and do the work. Our participation is vital!

> *The changes we're experiencing are not just physical. We are being energetically re-patterned. The status quo will no longer do.*

First, it's essential to cleanse our consciousness of the emotional poisons that glue us to the old paradigms in order to transmute ourselves to clarity, spaciousness, equanimity and wisdom. Learn to quiet the mind and listen to the voice of the heart. Discover the place of silence within that is in alignment with the heartbeat of the Earth and the galactic center. Burn away layers of mental, physical and emotional darkness and the core essence of love grows. Then, we are clear to live right action, truth and integrity—awake!

When working with students, I tell them that in nine months their lives will look and feel completely different. They often ask, "What does that mean?" With support, they take the most important step in exhuming their buried spirits from generations of anesthesia and moving them into the light. I don't have all the answers, but I do know that the work is to get our souls back on track. We are each living at this time on this planet for a specific reason. My work is to support individuals in discovering what that is.

In this time of spiritual renaissance, we each stand at a fork in the road. From the point of our choice to take one path or another, everything changes. If we take the status quo road, hoping and wanting everything to stay the same, we're in for pain and suffering. Great change is already occurring—there's no doubt about it. If we resist that change, it will bring us great stress and possibly even cause our demise.

> *In this time of spiritual renaissance, we each stand at a fork in the road. From the point of our choice to take one path or another, everything changes.*

On the other hand, if we choose to participate in the change by taking the road of self-transformation, we can create heaven on Earth. We'll be able to access magic, spontaneity, instantaneous manifestation, telepathy, time travel and much more. All the spiritual abilities we humans have suppressed in ourselves for eons are available to us. We'll realign with our light and earth bodies and reconnect with our divine source. This is who we truly are.

The great question we face as we approach 2012 is not, "What's happening?" but rather, "What am I doing?" Community consciousness and *we* connection is increasing, which is wonderful. The most important thing, however, is that we each focus on the *me*. As I change my consciousness, the *we*—the matrix, the planet, the universe—changes through the rippling, healing effect of our collective growth. In this time of great potential, conscious participation is vital. Nothing else will do.

Amirah Hall is an internationally renowned clairvoyant energy healer, speaker and teacher. After a near-death experience, Amirah's natural healing abilities and spiritual awareness were heightened and she has helped thousands of individuals world-wide gain clarity, balance, love and abundance in their lives. Her work encompasses physical, emotional and spiritual aspects that, when balanced, create harmony in one's life.

Amirah is the author of LOVE UP Your LIFE *and* WAKE UP! Shift Happens *and is the executive producer and host of* Lessons From THE LIGHT Radio. *Amirah has a master's degree in metaphysics, a bachelor's degree in business and over fifteen years of executive sales experience. She was born in Canada and resides in San Diego, California. (www.SoulMystic.com)*

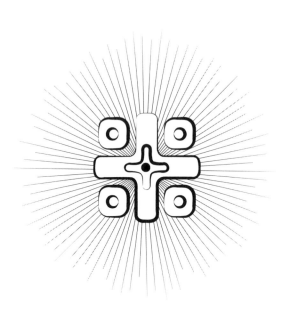

Paco Alarcon (Kahan)

A MESSAGE OF COMPASSION

The Great Mayan Prophecy says that 2012 may be the end of Earth time. This actually announces a period of freedom and expansion, liberated from the *limitations of time*. In a world of time, there is separation and karma. Consequently, the end of time is the end of separation and therefore the end of karma. For separation to end, people need to recover their power. The process toward the realization of the Mayan prophecy is a shift of power. It is an ascension process that takes people from ego power to divine power. It is about the change of consciousness that the recovery of power brings.

First, we need to look at what time is. Time is the way we have lived in this reality, a reality in which events happen and some consequences manifest. It is cause and effect. We can also call it karma. Cause needs time for effect to manifest. This is the world of time.

Beyond time, we have synchronicity: unity and love, a world without karma. Synchronicity requires a rise in the world's vibration, a shift which will accelerate processes until time collapses and synchronicity manifests. Thus we move from time to synchronicity, away from limitations and suffering and toward the reality of the Universe: joy and power. So this shift is about the end of the cause-and-effect reality and the manifestation of a reality of synchronicity. We need to qualify for that new reality.

The world we know is a project. I call it Project Earth. As a project, it has a beginning and an end. Life wasn't meant to be like this forever. It is not written anywhere. We had to come to the end of this project eventually, ending the world as we know it so we can enter a new world, a new way of living infused with that love and compassion the great masters taught.

2012 is a shift in consciousness awakened in divine power. It is a beautiful prophecy about possibilities, empowerment and light. We have to graduate to the spiritual level that takes us out of discipleship and into mastery. It is all about love, a graduation in love. The Mayan prophecy speaks about the end of time, and to prepare for that we need to raise our vibration. The moment we raise our vibration, we attain power. Once in possession of our true power, we move into *true compassion*. The end of time is thus the beginning of compassion. This is the secret code of the Great Mayan Prophecy.

Going to that state through our own graduation, we can create a reality of unity, love and compassion, and the new energies are pushing toward that reality. The Maya knew that, as 2012 approached, new energies would cause an acceleration that would bring an end to the cycle for Earth.

To ascend spiritually, we need to recover our power; ascension is the encounter with our spiritual reality, our true mastery. If power is not recovered, we experience dependency: serving other masters than ourselves, outside of our higher truth. This moves us away from mastery. We have seen that, as separation ends due to the end of time, karma disappears. The end of karma is the beginning of service. Compassion is the result of the end of karma, and the instrument for service. But we cannot be truly compassionate without power. So there is great urgency in the awakening consciousness of people to recover power. This is what the global crisis is about.

The end of separation is the beginning of love. Separation is the inner split keeping people away from their power, and therefore from their love. The end of separation is also the end of violence. Violence is the result of the use of ego power; when we use divine power, what we get is compassion.

Due to the high vibrational energies entering the Earth's field, people are going through a process of awakening to a new spiritual vibration that will eventually take everybody to this consciousness of compassion. Higher energies in a person awaken consciousness; greater light opens the heart. People are entering personal crisis because the energies are very strong, hitting everyone for a greater awakening of love through power. This changes our priorities and the way we live our lives.

> *The end of time is thus the beginning of compassion. This is the secret code of the Great Mayan Prophecy.*

So everybody is in some sort of crisis: existential crisis, financial crisis, relationship crisis, job crisis. Everybody is going through this, trying to make greater sense of their lives, because the modes of living they have understood until now are no longer valid; they don't make sense anymore. Opening the heart, entering the vibration of unconditional love and doing the right thing from love: this is the only thing that makes sense, and the only thing that works now. Acquiring and retaining one's own power is the only sensible thing to do during this shift. As I wrote in my book, *Stargate 2012: Recovering the Power for Earth's Imminent Ascension*: Your power is only yours; don't negotiate with it.

The moment we negotiate with our power, exchanging it for something else, we lose. Once power is lost, the door is open to any type of personal cataclysm. Power is our most precious possession. What we get in exchange for power is always less in value. And every time we negotiate with our power, we become less and less powerful—until we are finally at the mercy of external powers. 2012 is a door to a new reality of love, compassion and light. If we are ready we can take the opportunity. The Stargate that opens will allow us to enter into a new possibility of manifestation from new energies and make a creation from light, without limitations.

Power is the driving force of evolution. Without it all is stagnant: love, prosperity, relationships, spirituality. When we receive an awakening in power consciousness, we seek to recover power. Crisis is a call for power in the area where crisis is occurring. That takes us to a life crisis: a deep transformation in the way we think and act, and what we value—and the collapse of belief systems that give our power away. That deep transformation is an initiation, a spiritual awakening of huge proportions. Power recovery is the missing link in human beings. The process of ascension is therefore very clear: Elevate the vibrational frequencies where we have cast our power away.

> *Your power is only yours; don't negotiate with it.*

The awakening in power consciousness sends us on an intense walkabout within our depths, our dark side, for this is where power is being held hostage. The need to bring light to the dark areas inside of us is urgent now. When the dark side is not illuminated, its power serves a dark agenda; we may think we are very good, but our hearts are not truly open and our actions very often bring suffering and chaos. When the dark side is brought to the light, its power serves good. When power is separated, it is used for evil purposes. That split is the cause of all evil. Once the dark side is integrated, it serves the light. Only then are we truly good.

The ancient Maya were great beings, cosmic beings, visionaries able to see into the future and predict cycles. The ancient Maya opened the door out of time. For many years, spending time in some of the Mayan sites, I have been able to understand what goes on there: the sites are alive. The experience of high vibrations at the sites makes one feel completely out of time. The ancient Maya disappeared; they vanished. There are no remains of their presence other than their mysterious and enigmatic ruins in the middle of the jungle—and the high vibration they left behind. They set the record so we could follow it.

During the time I have worked in the Mayan sites, I have been there both with groups and alone for hours, surrounded by mystical ruins and fifth dimensional frequencies, connecting and anchoring higher energies. In silence, I have felt and heard a coded message, a silent presence that spoke of unity and peace, liberation and possibilities. I have been empowered by a mystical force that moved something in my energy codes, transforming me on some deep level. I was unable to explain it at the time, but I knew that something deep was happening. My energy in contact with Mayan energy unlocked ascension codes and revelations about the end of time. My work with these connections and revelations is explained in my book, *Stargate 2012*, and transmitted in my seminars.

> *The end of time, for the Maya, meant the end of a cycle. When a cycle turns to join the beginning in its closing finale, it's crucial that an increment of energy is added to create an evolutional spiral.*

The ancient Maya knew the implications of the end of time. But they left it to us to figure out the details. They knew where we were going with it, and that there would be a transition period between one reality and another—from low frequency to high frequency, from fear to love, and from a fear-based reality to a love-based world. The end of time, for the Maya, meant the end of a cycle. When a cycle turns to join the beginning in its closing finale, it's crucial that an increment of energy is added to create an evolutional spiral.

The world announced by the ancient Maya in their great prophecy is a world we can only go to by getting ready. The way to get ready is to raise our vibration—and take the right luggage: loving intentions, forgiveness and compassion. No excess weight is allowed in the new reality. This is the way to shift to the new paradigm. Compassion is the passport to ascension. It is the return of the Higher Self, the Christ. The illusion of separation between the superior consciousness and the lower consciousness disappears. The Mayan prophecy announces: "This is your opportunity to get ready for a new life, a new world of light. To be there you have to be luminous, hence no darkness in you." The question to ask is: Can you do that? Do you *want* to do that?

Recently, I spent some time in the Mayan sites, and again I was amazed at their power. There you can feel anything and be taken anywhere—because when time stops, you feel eternity. And that will always be a place of re-encounter with truth. The Mayan prophecy for 2012 is about the end of time: the beginning of compassion. In compassion, we are free.

Paco Alarcon (Kahan) is a world authority on the Mayan prophecy and the 2012 shift. At age sixteen, Kahan merged with universal consciousness, experiencing his own consciousness everywhere—the state many religions talk about. He has explored oriental and occidental spiritual currents for almost thirty years, gaining access to great spiritual revelations. During his work of many years in Mayan sites, he unlocked energy codes for ascension and the shift in 2012. In his seminars, Kahan makes spiritual experiences very accessible, putting people in direct contact with their true essence and a high vibrational energy that transforms their lives. His aim is to unite the power of Spirit with day-to-day life, bringing people closer to the real experience of God.

Kahan is the author of three books: Stargate 2012: Recovering the Power for Earth's Imminent Ascension; The Violet Light: The Power That Changes Everything; *and* Flying Within, *a novel about personal paradigm change. He is also a composer of jazz and high-vibrational music. His concerts and CDs impact audiences deeply and expand their light. To learn more about Kahan, visit www.Kahan.eu.*

Dr. Gabriel Cousens

THE CULTURE OF LIFE
AND LIBERATION

The year 2012 is neither a singular nor a potential turning point. It is, rather, part of a massive shift we are experiencing even now. It is a very profound shift, toward a "Culture of Life and Liberation" for all the beings on our planet.

We are in the process of awakening from a culture of death, represented by economic exploitation of all humans, animals and the living planet, through such dark entities as the Federal Reserve, the FDA and the IRS. This culture of death has been treating the planet as if it were a store going out of business; however, we are moving into what we call the Culture of Life and Liberation, where love, compassion, interrelatedness and God become the center of our lives. It requires our collective cooperation to shift the planetary forces of consciousness into the Culture of Life and Liberation.

This time is about increasing the resonance and expanding the power of light to transform this world in every way. It means a return to natural food, natural medicine and natural trading systems. It will involve, on some level, a fragmentation and reordering of all nations in a way that brings peace, prosperity and quality of life to all the people on the planet. This movement, which has already begun, will experience a shift in 2012, ultimately stabilizing in 2039.

People tend to create dark fantasies around dates. In 1979, my family was living off the grid in Mendocino, California. There was a big scare, but nothing happened. Again in 1989 and at Y2K, we saw a build-up of fear followed by the absence of worldwide catastrophe. I believe that the same brand of mass negative fantasy may be happening with 2012. Having been through it so many times now, my position is quite positive.

> It requires our collective cooperation to shift the planetary forces of consciousness into the Culture of Life and Liberation.

The Hopi prophecies of the Fifth World (humanity's next phase) do not state a specific date. They do say that very soon we will move from being "two-hearted" people to being "one-hearted" people. An Earth-centered, peace-bringing group is evolving right now. This group will positively and lovingly transform the planet. What this means, in a very practical sense, is that we do not have to be perfect, but we will have to renew the energies of *true* morality and modesty. We have to live in harmony with all four levels of beings on the planet: the sprouting ones, the walking ones, the flying ones and the speaking ones.

A planetary alignment will occur on December 21, 2012. It will be similar to the planetary alignment that occurred in the Harmonic Convergence of 1987. That convergence resulted in the downfall of the Russian Empire and the Berlin Wall. I was among three thousand people at a twenty-four-hour gathering on Sonoma Mountain, where we all were meditating, chanting and dancing. Millions of people around the world holding this focus simultaneously, created a positive energetic wave that, we believe, brought down those oppressive empires and symbols. It followed in a couple of years, but it happened. These cosmic events are relevant, but they are relevant in terms of how we work with the energies.

The dark side and the dark cabal have been the dominant forces on the planet for thousands of years. A few years ago, while dancing four days in the Spirit Dance (the Lakota Ghost Dance), subsisting on only water, I was among those who received a vision of the future. In this vision, 2012–2013 was to be a nodal turning point in the strengthening of the Culture of Life and Liberation. 2025–2026 will also be a major turning point during which the Forces of Life and Liberation will become *stronger* than the culture of death. Finally, 2039 will mark a more serious stabilization of the Culture of Life and Liberation.

The culture of death has already lost the war, but it has a few battles left. Therefore, the most important shift we can make is in *consciousness*. We are experiencing an onslaught of poisonous energies and substances. However, people have become less willing to accept the dulling of their "five-sense bio-computer minds." Chemtrails, mass vaccinations, genetically modified food, frequency devices and radiated food, all, I believe, decrease brain function. People are acting to preserve their precious human organisms, so that they can transcend them and awaken.

> *The culture of death has already lost the war, but it has a few battles left.*

An example of this very active intelligence can be witnessed right now. According to some surveys, more than seventy-five percent of parents do not wish to vaccinate their children with an untested, possibly very dangerous swine flu vaccine. Although the dark cabal is saying everybody should be vaccinated, they are not telling us what the vaccine contains. In 1976, more people died from Guillain-Barré syndrome, *caused by* the swine flu vaccine, than they did from the flu itself. A big sign of this shift is that people are getting wise to the fact that our so-called leaders are not necessarily giving us the best advice. This is happening now. We are not waiting for 2012.

Seventy-five percent of parents, fifty percent of doctors and sixty percent of nurses in the United States are refusing to be vaccinated. This is not a medical statement. This is about people listening to their hearts and letting themselves be intuitively guided through what is happening. They are refusing to be inoculated with a live virus that is contagious for three weeks. They are refusing those extremely high levels of mercury. They are refusing squalene, the chemical that caused three-hundred-thousand vets to be totally disabled by Gulf War Syndrome and which is one million times more concentrated in the H1N1 vaccine. An H1N1 flu virus was lab-created. This information has been publicly released in reports from the Center for Disease Control.

> *This is about people listening to their hearts and letting themselves be intuitively guided through what is happening.*

Codex Alimentarius, a move by the World Health Organization, is trying—with success in some countries—to outlaw supplements, organic farming (including personal gardening), vitamins and natural and organic foods. They have already succeeded in setting allowable limits of seven major pesticides, carcinogens that were outlawed in the past; they have tried two bills in the US that, fortunately, did not pass.

We know that organic, living food is a key to good health, and that poisoned food creates a dysfunctional nervous system. The average child today has over two hundred neurotoxins in his blood. That means the average kid has a lot of problems with everything from hyperactivity to autism, which may later become Parkinson's and/or Alzheimer's disease. (According to Dan Olmstead, author of *The Age of Autism*, it is no accident that the Amish have no cases of autism—they do not allow vaccinations.) However, the average child who eats organic food has one-quarter to one-sixth the amount of toxins in his or her blood. Codex Alimentarius, and the H1N1 virus and vaccine, are direct outreach from the dark side.

The good news is that there is vigorous resistance to the dark side. People are beginning to return to more natural ways of living. People are reconnecting with the truth of their intuition, believing in the Culture of Life and Liberation rather than the messages from the culture of death motivated by profit and exploitation. This shift is happening *right now.*

People aren't buying into the lies anymore. They are waking up from Numbsville and learning to take care of themselves. Using tools such as toxins and the H1N1 vaccine, the dark forces are able to project fear, terror and separation into people's minds. People cannot make right decisions. The 2012 energy, as we have seen with the vaccine situation, signifies this *shift.* People are moving away from that fear, and into a positivity that will allow them to make higher-level decisions about their lives. As we live a modest, moral and integrated life, we start making decisions that uplift ourselves *and* the planet. Though meditating, creating a positive energy field around ourselves and doing good deeds sounds simple, it will be absolutely essential to profoundly healing ourselves and the world.

> People aren't buying into the lies anymore.
> They are waking up from Numbsville and
> learning to take care of themselves.

Time is speeding up and moving so fast that we have to move from left brain to right brain. We are being forced to become more intuitive in order to take in the amazing amount of information we are receiving. Ultimately, life is simple. Start every act with love. Start every sentence with the seed of love, peace and interrelatedness. Move your thoughts and words into positive actions. Maybe we can start with fifty-one percent positive actions and move to sixty, seventy, eighty percent. This is already happening.

The most important thing you can do right now is open your heart to the Divine, and let that guide you to where you are meant to be. Let that guide you through your life's circumstances. From a higher perspective, all that is happening is a shift in consciousness. We have a bright future ahead of us as the Culture of Life and Liberation. The door is already open.

Doctor Sir Rabbi Gabriel Cousens MD, MD(H), DD, Diplomate of the American Board of Integrative Holistic Medicine, Diplomate Ayurveda, Native American Sundancer and Spirit Dance chief, visionary mystic and founder and director of The Tree of Life Rejuvenation Center and Tree of Life Foundation (www.TreeOfLife.nu), is a leading author, world-renowned spiritual teacher, holistic physician and a leading live-food medical expert.

Gabriel's books include: There Is A Cure for Diabetes; Spiritual Nutrition: Six Foundations for Spiritual Life and the Awakening of Kundalini; Rainbow Green Live-Food Cuisine; Conscious Eating; Depression-Free for Life; Tachyon Energy *and* Creating Peace by Being Peace: An Essene Sevenfold Path.

Gabriel has been involved in humanitarian work since 1963, teaches in dozens of countries around the world and has recently created an international online community at www.GabrielCousens.com.

Laura Dunham, PhD

SPIRITUAL WISDOM FOR 2012

A friend asked recently, "What's all the fuss about 2012? Is it another Y2K—much ado about nothing—or is something big really going to happen?" Good question. An explosion of books, TV documentaries, articles, movies and YouTube videos invites us to explore conflicting and confusing prophecies and predictions about the significance of December 21, 2012.

Will this long-anticipated date signal the tipping point of a transformational shift in human consciousness? Spiritual leaders and followers of the Mayan calendar, ancient prophecies and cosmic messages say *yes*. Some, citing the Book of Revelation or the latest UFO or conspiracy theory, predict Doomsday. Meanwhile, scientists and environmentalists warn of impending natural and eco-disasters: climate change, species extinction, basic resource shortages leading to mass migration and pandemics—to name just a few. The global economic crisis and escalating geopolitical conflicts add to the threats faced by humanity and the planet in our lifetimes. Life on planet Earth is changing dramatically and rapidly.

Specifically what may happen on December 21, 2012, is unclear, but indications are that a period of intense solar storms peaking in 2011 and 2012 will play havoc with the electromagnetic fields of Earth and her creatures. These storms have the potential to disrupt telecommunications, human and animal behavior and even precipitate a pole shift. In addition, a rare alignment of the Earth and Sun with the dark rift at the center of the Milky Way galaxy will occur around the winter solstice of 2012, the consequences of which are open to speculation. Adding to the debate, Swedish scientist Carl Johan Calleman links the Mayan calendar to the evolution of human consciousness and cites October 28, 2011, as the date when a quantum leap through time will end in a fully evolved humanity. If he is right, those focusing on December 2012 will be out of sync with the calendar.

Whatever happens on the path to 2012 and beyond, it is increasingly clear that humanity is at a crossroads and must envision and co-create a sustainable future. At 6.7 billion and counting, the world's population is rapidly outpacing and destroying our planet's capacity to support us along with other forms of life. Soon we won't have a choice about our future. To co-create the most hopeful outcome for ourselves and our planet, we must direct our consciousness and actions toward the highest good of all.

As a spiritual energy healer and teacher, I know that our thoughts and intentions take energetic form and connect with energy fields vibrating at similar frequencies. As more people move through their own consciousness shifts, connecting head and heart with Universal Creative Intelligence (God or Spirit), our collective vibration will elevate to higher, finer frequencies. It is conceivable that when a critical mass reaches that level of resonance, the lower frequencies of fear, greed and hate will no longer prevail.

As the collective consciousness transforms, radical changes in belief systems and lifestyles occur quickly. Through silent meditation, musical frequencies, spiritual energy healing and other means known to scientists and spiritual teachers, people begin to experience the magnificence of our multi-dimensional universe. The fully conscious human sees life throughout the cosmos as interconnected and purposeful; each life forms a unique expression of universal intelligence, creativity and love. Love constantly seeks relationship, creating new expressions and combinations of energy that shift and flow. Now a wave, now a particle, the frequencies and vibrations of the energy combine in unique ways, forming seemingly random patterns endlessly unique and yet linked in geometric patterns. Networks and systems emerge that support the level of vibration or consciousness held by each life form, including the human.

> It is conceivable that when a critical
> mass reaches that level of resonance,
> the lower frequencies of fear, greed
> and hate will no longer prevail.

Having experienced my own consciousness shift, I began to teach others how to access this path and to offer spiritual energy healing for people, places and the planet. Out of my years of research and experience, I wrote *Spiritual Wisdom for a Planet in Peril: Preparing for 2012 and Beyond*, a book to guide people through these turbulent times without fear and to help them prepare on many levels for a world transformed. As I began work on the book, I gathered sixteen fellow spiritual healers and teachers in January 2008 on Epiphany weekend for a conversation on 2012 prophecies and possibilities. Epiphany celebrates the birth of the Christ Consciousness on the planet, long awaited by ancient Wise Ones, so the timing was auspicious. Christ or Unity Consciousness provides a blueprint for human transformation during this new Aquarian Age. Over two days, our conversation ranged from the Mayan calendar's map of evolving human consciousness to scientific and spiritual predictions of Earth and human-caused changes. We discussed the signs of the times and discerned the most probable scenarios on the path through 2012. Finally, we outlined the actions required now to support the most hopeful future for our planet.

Although it's important to focus first on what the signs of the times reveal and the most significant prophecies and possibilities surrounding 2012, all too often that is where the conversation stops.

Predictions of disasters capture the popular imagination and media, while efforts to support consciousness shifts draw less attention. It is time to widen the conversation, both to help people prepare for what lies ahead and to engage a broader audience so that more will be ready. In my book I demonstrate how to:

- envision a new way of being
- strengthen our spiritual connections
- choose supportive locations and lifestyles
- thrive in a sustainable economy
- create intentional community and
- develop an action plan

As we take these steps we will cross the threshold of 2012 as humanity transformed into a world of harmony, abundance and peace. By working together for the highest good of our planet and ourselves, we will find the support we need. New initiatives and projects are being co-created by people of good will every day and are manifesting more quickly than ever.

> *As we approach 2012, all of us have the power to shape our own destinies and to join together to co-create with our thoughts, intentions and actions a world that reflects our collective consciousness.*

An organization I helped birth, Power of One: Become the Change/Transform the World, has taken shape rapidly and expanded in scope as people are drawn to its vision. Our Power of One team aspires to bring people together on October 10, 2010, on the Mall in Washington, DC, linked with sites around the world, to inspire and empower people to take personal responsibility and join together as one to co-create solutions to humanity's greatest challenges. A year of quantum dialogues precedes this event and leads to the kinds of quantum actions needed now.

The world is changing. Already old paradigm systems, largely hierarchical and male-dominated—governments, economies, religious institutions, educational and health care systems—are morphing into higher consciousness, life-giving, inclusive forms of human expression. People are creating new alliances, both locally and at a distance, that serve their needs without exploiting the natural environment. Our relationship with Earth and her creatures as well as cosmic forces is changing profoundly. As we approach 2012, all of us have the power to shape our own destinies and to join together to co-create with our thoughts, intentions and actions a world that reflects our collective consciousness.

> *We will no longer see ourselves as separated by race, gender, nationality or religion, but rather as expressions of the One—Source Energy—united in love at ever more complex levels of being.*

In preparing for the consciousness shift that accompanies the period surrounding 2012, we are becoming explorers of both inner and outer space, venturing into the unknown on the physical planet and the cosmos as well as within ourselves. The Information Age is giving way to the Age of Wisdom, as knowledge balanced by love becomes a powerful tool to propel humanity through the shift. No longer will we misuse our gifts of knowledge for selfish purposes, such as power and wealth for the few. In human history, that perversion of the natural order destroyed civilizations. Instead, we will join with collaborative partners in many realms in ventures that support all life.

Emerging partnerships and communities grow out of our realized connection with Universal Creative Intelligence. Nothing is more important as we prepare for the cosmic shift than our personal spiritual connections. By developing and exploring these connections; expanding our spiritual knowledge and practices; doing our inner work and integrating and applying our knowledge and wisdom to a new way of living in unity consciousness, we will be ready for whatever comes. We will no longer see ourselves as separated by race, gender, nationality or religion, but rather as expressions of the One—Source Energy—united in love at ever more complex levels of being.

When we trust that we can find the answers we seek and create the opportunities and support systems we desire, life on the path through 2012 becomes less frightening and more appealing and exciting. We have much to look forward to as we continue to transform through 2012!

Dr. Laura Dunham is the author of five books, including Spiritual Wisdom for a Planet in Peril: Preparing for 2012 and Beyond. *Laura has spent a lifetime helping people make life-enhancing decisions. Throughout her careers in higher education, financial planning and ordained ministry, she has been a recognized healer. A Certified Financial Planner for twenty-one years, Laura counseled hundreds of clients and appeared frequently in* Money *and* The Wall Street Journal.

A former pastor, her specialties in ministry were financial and environmental stewardship, mission and spiritual development. Laura was commissioned by the Ecumenical Stewardships Center to write Graceful Living: Your Faith, Values, and Money in Changing Times *(2002). In addition to BA, MA, MDiv and PhD degrees, she holds a certificate in Spiritual Formation. As a media commentator and spiritual energy healer, Laura shares her expertise with audiences worldwide; her work and interests have taken her to more than forty countries. Laura helped birth* Power of One: Become the Change/Transform the World *(www.PowerOfOne.org). She invites readers to join the conversation through her blog, www.2012isComing.com. To learn more about Laura, visit www.HealingAndWisdom.com.*

Shared by *Jelaila Starr*

PREPARING FOR A
NEW AGE OF LIGHT
A MESSAGE FROM THE NIBIRUANS

Nibiru, the twelfth planet of our solar system, has a thirty-six-hundred-year orbit. It has been recorded in the writings and carvings of ancient civilizations from Egypt and India to Mesopotamia and South America. The Nibiruans first visited Earth four-hundred-eighty-thousand years ago. They are not only multi-racial; they are also from many species.

The Nibiruans claim to have created humankind two-hundred-sixty-two-thousand years ago, thus becoming our parent race. They have been off-planet for over four-thousand years, but have not abandoned us. Rather, they have been watching over us and our evolutionary journey since our inception. As we approach our spiritual graduation, the Nibiruans, through one of their spiritual leaders and designated spokespersons, Devin, send a heartfelt and loving message.

Greetings:
It is with great joy that we deliver this message. We are the Nibiruans, people from a distant world who, in our quest to save our planet, discovered your world. We did not know at the time that our mission would lead us to create a new species or that, in doing so, we would fulfill our own divine destiny as a parent race. It wasn't until some time after we first created you that we learned your true nature and destiny from our ancient elders. Through you, a new seed race can be created, one that can achieve compassion and thus peace. That

is your divine destiny: to populate the galaxy with a compassionate species that can live—and teach others how to live—peacefully, in harmony with diversity.

Per your mission, you have reached the point at which you are ready for ascension; so commences the final phase of your evolution on a third-dimensional world. Your ascension coincides with the return of our planet into your sector, your planet's crossing of the galactic equator at the end of a grand galactic cycle, and the dawn of a new thirteen-thousand-year age of light. What a grand time to graduate!

We began our efforts to assist in this final phase when we provided the knowledge of how to realign, reconnect and activate (recode) your ten dormant strands of DNA. Yes, we disconnected them. For two reasons: First, we created you with stellar twelve-strand DNA. This means that you carry the codes for all species in our universe. In other words, you are a living library. Such a species is frequently sought after by other off-world groups in order to create new, more advanced races. Second, as a species with natural telepathy and technological prowess, yet still young and somewhat innocent, you were often duped into situations that threatened your survival. Your biblical tale of the Tower of Babel was one such event and much more involved than you have been told.

Though we policed these situations, we could not stop them all. Recognizing the gravity of the whole picture, we decided that the best way to ensure your survival was to disconnect many of your gifts. Not only did we disconnect ten of your DNA strands, we encrypted them so that no one could reassemble your DNA until you had reached spiritual maturity. True to our word, we have given you the key and a process that, together, will decrypt and recompile your DNA in a manner that restores your former abilities and gifts. The key is the *Formula of Compassion,* and the process is DNA Recoding. The nine steps of the Formula of Compassion are key to decrypting and unlocking DNA. These steps activate the thymus at the ninth dimensional level, causing it to transmute negative energy into compassion.

Do you wonder why you are being observed by a multitude of galactic worlds as you usher in a new age of light? Your divine mission involved a grand experiment. I'll explain.

> *The nine steps of the Formula of Compassion*
> *are key to decrypting and unlocking DNA.*
> *These steps activate the thymus at the ninth*
> *dimensional level, causing it to transmute*
> *negative energy into compassion.*

In our universe, there's a game for "soul evolution." We call it a game because souls, being creator gods/goddesses, learn best through structured systems that allow us to create. Then, through built-in challenges, souls learn to master our creations. Soul games are the highest, most sacred form of game. In this universe, we play the Polarity Integration Game, a game that requires our learning to integrate, or accept as equally valuable, all aspects of the Light and Dark polarities. Eventually, we reach the point wherein our creations can literally destroy us and our universe. That is when the spiritual hierarchy sets aside a planet and quarantines it for the purpose of integration.

Over time, all galactic worlds participating in the experiment will send their people to the host planet either through contributing DNA, as in the case of your creation two-hundred-sixty-two-thousand years ago, or through entering the planet's birth cycle. Either method will ensure that the timelines of these worlds, along with those of previously destroyed worlds, are woven into the timeline of the host planet.

With all the timelines interwoven, any healing completed will have a ripple effect on all the timelines, healing the past... and the future, since all time is now. With all timelines healed, the game ends; the souls move on to other universes to engage in more advanced soul games in order to continue their evolution.

Once we became aware of your divine nature and destiny, we consciously strove to help you evolve and fulfill your purpose. Our planet Nibiru became the Galactic Federation's field office for those participating in the Grand Experiment. Delegates from participating worlds live here, and call it their "home away from home."

We have worked, and will continue to work, with the most enlightened beings from all across the galaxy and in the non-incarnate realms. The list includes, but is not limited to, your ancient ancestors from Lyra, the Felines of Sirius A, the Cetaceans of Sirius C, the Pleiadians (both human and reptilian), Arcturians, Andromedans and members of the Christos Office on Venus who work in concert with the Hathors and the Kumaras of Orion and Sirius B. Together, we have monitored your progress by sending leaders, teachers and prophets such as Pharoah Akhenaten, Moses, Buddha, Jesus and Mohammed to guide and enlighten you.

> *Soul games are the highest, most sacred form of game. In this universe, we play the Polarity Integration Game, a game that requires our learning to integrate, or accept as equally valuable, all aspects of the Light and Dark polarities.*

Additionally, we work on all the timelines. Those include the demise of four worlds, two of which were previous failed Grand Experiments. The events of those timelines are the stuff of which your ancient prophecies are made. The final days of each of those destroyed worlds are, and will continue to be, played out on your world until the end of 2012. This brings me to the point about compassion and your divine mission and destiny.

As your planet crosses the galactic equator, you will move through a field of very high pro-evolutionary energy emanating from the galactic core, called a galactic superwave. As you move deeper into the field where the vibration is much faster, your thoughts and feelings will instantly manifest.

Each of you carries not only emotional pain from your present incarnation, but the pain of your ancient past on Earth and beyond as well. That pain is buried in every cell of your body and imprinted in your DNA. Your mission is to heal as much of the pain as you can before the end of 2012, when your planet enters the deeper regions of the field. When this is accomplished, you will create a new reality in alignment with your highest potential, a world where compassionate and peaceful people live in harmony with diversity.

That's why each of you needs to prepare your own consciousness for 2012. The consciousness you have on this side of the galactic equator is the one you'll have on the other side, only it'll be greatly amplified.

This is why you are having seemingly insurmountable challenges now. The intensity is required to shake you out of your comfort zones in order to integrate deep-seated fears and clear out old traumas at a new level that enables you to achieve compassion. This means releasing any feelings of victimhood and taking full responsibility. That's why each of you needs to prepare your own consciousness for 2012. The consciousness you have on this side of the galactic equator is the one you'll have on the other side, only it'll be greatly amplified.

We, your parent race, have faith that through the challenges ahead you will awaken to your true identity and your divine purpose. Know that we love you and will continue to walk beside you as we have since your birth. And remember, you are the hope of the universe.

Jelaila Starr experienced a spiritual awakening in 1992 and thus began the spiritual path. In 1995, she was awakened to the knowledge of her walk-in, and began DNA Recoding soon after. Having completed her training and DNA Recoding in late 1996, Jelaila embarked upon her mission as a galactic historian, channel and messenger for the Nibiruans.

The Nibiruan Council was founded in early 1997 as a vehicle through which Jelaila publishes the Nibiruans' writings on the higher knowledge of DNA Recoding, as well as the bigger picture of our galactic and universal history. This knowledge, coupled with Jelaila's simple and down-to-earth approach, enables her to reach across the boundaries of belief systems that separate our world to provide insight, understanding, hope and, most importantly, a concrete formula for self-empowerment. To learn more about Jelaila and the Nibiruan Council, please visit www.NibiruanCouncil.com.

Sergio Magaña and Chrystelle Hadjikakou

2010: FAST-FORWARD ON THE TIMES

Our sun has set; our sun has hidden and has left us in utter darkness. However, we know that he shall rise again to cast his light upon us. While he remains there, in Miktlan, the land of the dead, we must unite and hide all that we love within our hearts. Let us hide our temples (Teokaltin), our schools (Kalmekak), our game fields (Telpoxkaltin), and our houses of song (Kuikakaltin). Let us leave the streets deserted and lock ourselves in our houses; it is there that we shall find our teokaltin, our kalmekak, our telpoxkaltin, our kuikakaltin, from now on and until the new sun rises. The fathers and mothers shall be the teachers and guides who shall lead their children by the hand while they live; let the fathers and mothers never forget to tell their children what has until now been Anahuac, protected by the gods and the result of the good customs and education that our ancestors have taught us with such perseverance. Let them not forget to tell their children how one day, this land shall rise to become Anahuac once more, the land of the new sun.

–The Directive of the Mexicayotl, passed on from Cuauhtemoc.

This time has come. Despite the worldwide publicity around December 21, 2012, we believe that these are calculations for the Great Awakening of the Mayan region. As important as this date is for the global cosmic evolution in other parts of the world, other dates hold a greater weight, at least with respect to immediate changes. This is the case in the Valley of Anahuac.

The Valley of Anahuac includes the areas of Mexico City and its surroundings and, according to the Tepeyolotl (high priests of the mountains), is bordered by cosmic mountains that divide the Mexican territory into several regions. According to ancient tradition, this area is not ruled by the Tzolkin (the Mayan calendar), but by the Tonalpohualli, the Aztec calendar which has been inherited from the ancestors of Anahuac, the Toltecs and the Teotihuacans, and whose count system has proven, to this day, to be fully valid in this geographic region.

Although the Aztecs (Mexicas) have generally been considered bloodthirsty and barbaric due to their practice of human sacrifices, they were in reality a highly advanced civilization, a culture that developed spirituality so greatly that they did not need to develop machinery of any sort—everything gravitated around spiritual growth and the development of an awareness that needs to be awakened once more. As the clock carries on ticking, the need for the return of the Mexicas to their land grows ever greater.

The Aztec calendar contains information on the natural cycles of the planet. The computing of these cycles, known as the Nahui Ollin or the "Four Movements," interprets all existence, including the natural cycles of the great cosmic clock in four phases and their corresponding duality or "nighttime." The duration of the Earth's rotation on its axis marks the days; the duration of the orbit defines the seasons; the moon's cycles mark the months; and the great movements of the constellations measure centuries, millennia and eras.

The Aztecs called the great force that moves the entire universe "Centiuctli," the sole owner of the All, who manifests in all creation through dual combinations. This duality was recognized as a cosmic constant named "Ometeotl." Ometeotl, as it applies to itself, gave way to the Supreme Law of the Cosmos, or the Four Movements, which gives four phases to every cycle, no matter how large or small. While one cycle ends, the next is already beginning, and it is this combination of both energies that generates the conditions for the next cycle. So, just before a century changes, the new generation is born and eventually reaches a point of balance during the first decade of the new century, absorbing the cosmic legacy from the last. However, the generation that ends its reign resists this change, and the second decade of each century is when the energies of the next period are defined.

> *For Anahuac, the greatest period*
> *of transformation is now.*

It is during one such transition period that the Aztec empire was conquered; during another, Mexico became an independent nation; and exactly one hundred years later, history repeated itself with the Revolution. In 2010, Mexico shall complete yet another count of this cycle, deeply immersed in transformation as the cosmic and solar axes align themselves to mark a major cosmic event.

For Anahuac, the greatest period of transformation is now. The valley of Anahuac, surrounded by the mountains of four converging ranges that watch over the land in an intricate array of energy lines which need to be activated by those who remember the ancient traditions, also holds within itself the heart of a greater region. According to the prophecy, the heart needs to beat before anything can happen anywhere; Anahuac needs to be awoken once more; and the awareness that has gradually been lost since the conquest must be gained anew.

The Aztecs, who created one of the greatest known empires, were a society of spiritual warriors who had reached incredibly high levels of mind, spirit and body mastery. They did this through physical exercise; the human body naturally rejects carrying heavy weights, but through the development of the mind, they lightened objects to the point of levitating them. They used the same technique to fly, which is why the masters of these techniques were called "eagle warriors." A society as highly developed as this could have fought the conquistadors; however, they were aware of the prophecy. It said that, in order to create the conditions for a global awakening, they would have to allow the barbarians to take over their land. This would create a necessary rift between man and nature and a disorderly growth of the population to facilitate the gathering of seventy million people, both native and foreign, for the Great Ritual of the year 2021, when the sixth sun would finally enter its reign.

> *Everything is linked in a chain of events that began hundreds of years ago, joining the efforts of generations of people throughout the globe.*

This event, however, depends on several key stages, one of which we are living through now. The fifth sun was one of darkness, in which every spiritual development in America was erased. The sixth sun is one of rebirth, which entered Anahuac in 1991; the climax of its entrance will occur during the total solar eclipse of July 11, 2010, a date when everyone who knows of the prophecy must celebrate a ritual to awaken the heart of Mexico, located in the Great Temple (Templo Mayor) of Mexico City. This will begin the preparation for the Great Ritual of 2021, in which seventy million people concentrated around Mexico City are to welcome the full entering of the sixth sun and the opening of the path to the stars, where we will recover our star memory; the contact is prophesied to begin in Venus, home to the energy of Quetzalcoatl, the god of light.

Everything is linked in a chain of events that began hundreds of years ago, joining the efforts of generations of people throughout the globe. Aware of their part in this grand scheme, and to avoid being enslaved in their own land, the eagle and jaguar warriors decided to commit suicide without presenting opposition to the conquistadors. Today, the task is as momentous as it was in their time.

We are transitioning from a time referred to as a "sun of darkness" by the Mexicas, a cycle of 6,625 years that corresponds to the autumn of humanity. In this time, violence and destruction are prevalent and the sacred knowledge surfaces only briefly, to be quenched again by other cultures. However, the 2012 transition heralds the coming of the "sun of light," the sixth sun, which enters full force in 2021 and brings 6,625 years of spiritual growth and the coming of the new humanity, in rhythm with the laws of nature. This new cycle promises new possibilities with different, more luminous outcomes for all.

> *This new cycle promises new possibilities with different, more luminous outcomes for all.*

The opening of the sacred Aztec knowledge, just like the eclipse in 2010, is as indispensable for the return of the Tlatoani, the "carriers of the word," as the shift in awareness from the scientific-logical mind to the spiritual mind. These are all parts of a chain of events, not the end of them. Should these events be successful, the world could once more receive the Pleiadean vibration, and re-establish the brotherhood that was lost between the twelve Star Nations, our Sun and our Earth.

These are the words of the Tlatoani, the keepers of this knowledge of the great Aztec Calendar.

Sergio Magaña is a healer, author, leading expert on Mexica and Toltec paths and an initiate in the Andean, Toltec and Mexica paths. Through his studies with the keepers of these hidden wisdoms, Sergio developed bioenergetic healing techniques that defy the paradigms set by science and social beliefs, helping more than ten thousand patients achieve amazing results and transcend limitations. In 2000, he began hosting the radio program 2010: Fast-Forward on Time – 2012: The Days to Come. *In his workshops, Sergio has guided more than thirty thousand students toward great leaps in the development of consciousness as they experience impressive phenomena while healing the journey of their souls. Learn more about Sergio at www. ConcienciaDimensional.com, and his blog: 2010FastForwardTime. blog.com.*

Chrystelle Hadjikakou is a healer, teacher, filmmaker, writer and initiate in the Scandinavian, Toltec and Andean paths. She co-hosts the radio program 2012: Fast-Forward on Time – 2012: The Days to Come, *performs healings and teaches workshops on spiritual and emotional growth worldwide. A Fourth-Level Andean Priestess, Chrystelle translated Elizabeth Jenkins's* The Return of the Inka *and* Journey to Q'eros *into Spanish and German (2009/2010), and is currently working on her book,* Awakening to Our Inheritance: Prophecies Don't Fulfill Themselves. *Learn more about Chrystelle at EarthMysteries.blog.co.uk.*

Brenda Black

CHARTING THE DAY

It is said that the Meso-American Mayan calendar, which has three systems for counting days: the Tzolkin, Long Count and Haab, had its official beginning on August 11, 3114 BC. The calculated end of the full cycle of the Mayan calendar will be on December 21, 2012.

What is before you is not in support of a theory of doom and gloom, or of catastrophe. Rather, the following is a professional astrological interpretation of not only the chart for the day December 21, 2012, but also a chart for the next 5,125 years! This is the time of the alignment of the December solstice sun with the galactic equator, which will take place at 11:12 AM Greenwich time.

The Sun will be at zero degrees of Capricorn, and common everyday life may become more difficult for the residents of the global community as we struggle through the continued great recession. Environmental pollution, global warming and other changes to the Earth will continue. As these times turn increasingly stressful, people of all walks of life will pair up, not necessarily as marriage partners, but rather into cosmic unions with each other as friends, family members and networking associates, while observing and experiencing the world as it transcends into a new era.

With the Moon and Mercury in a friendly aspect to one another, the Internet community will be alive and well. Actually, a global community is evolving where the best traits and traditions of each culture are blending, making us all citizens of the world. Pisces ascendant and Neptune rising indicate that the human race is evolving into a new species that, over the next five centuries, will be attuned to galactic whispers and messages from the universe. We are evolving into our light bodies, and we are becoming increasingly psychic and intuitive. Our gifted and amazingly psychic indigo and crystal children are the forerunners of this era.

> *Because the Mayan calendar may have been created with the synergy of galactic beings* and *Maya natives, perhaps these intelligent minds will once again have direct or indirect contact with humans at this time.*

There is a Yod bringing in the energies of Jupiter in Gemini, Saturn in Scorpio and Pluto in Capricorn at 8 degrees respectively. A Yod (also called the Finger of God) is a formation of three planets in an astrology chart that accelerate fate, and it seems an irritating situation may arise which can only be overcome through adaptation, compromise and the discovery of a new solution.

The principles of transformation, rebirth and powerful actions are with us on December 21, 2012, and into the future. This is a time when Mother Earth is ripe and ready for a very fated change and a predestined new outlook. We must look toward a different path for survival. Although this new path may arrive abruptly, we have been preparing for it for many years. There is a new, unaccustomed focus that appears, but surprisingly, humans will accept it and move right along with it. The apex of the Yod is Jupiter in Gemini. This brings about new communication networks and whole new concepts of employment. Because the Mayan calendar may have been created with the synergy of galactic beings *and* Maya natives, perhaps these intelligent minds will once again have direct or indirect contact with humans at this time.

Each planet in the Yod is aligned with significant fixed stars. Jupiter at 8 degrees of Gemini is aligned with Aldebaran, one of the greatest fixed stars in the sky. This gives an implication of further aggressive military action around the world at the beginning of this new 5,125-year era. Then, later on, there will be an advanced form of population protection and control that is tied in with spiritual values. Saturn is close to the fixed star Alphecca (also called Corona Borealis) that signifies a crown of flowers. This suggests that good things come after a period of strife.

Into the year 2012, there will be more military action and suffering on the planet, which will most likely last for another one hundred years. And then, once again, there will be a more peaceful, agrarian energy on the planet.

> *Basically, life will remain the same as it is for most of us on that particular day. The great calamity depicted in the media will not occur. Banks will be open and the buses will still be running.*

Pluto at 8 degrees of Capricorn is aligned with the fixed star Facies that depicts the victim of the archer's aim, or the penetrating stare of a lethal weapon. This image will last longer than most think, but life goes on—many will feel hardship, as they have for the last millennium, but those who have a strong focus on their goals and a lifestyle of self-sufficiency will still achieve their dreams. Basically, life will remain the same as it is for most of us on that particular day. The great calamity depicted in the media will not occur. Banks will be open and the buses will still be running.

The South Node at 24 degrees of Taurus in the December 21, 2012, chart is connected to Caput Algol, which is the fixed star of damage to neck and throat, fires, sickness, violence, murder and horror. Algol gives voice to the passion of the common people and is connected to the sexual elements in society, which may mean a wider spreading of sexually transmitted diseases.

Looking at the Sibly chart of the United States, Jupiter will sit at 8 degrees of Gemini conjuncting the Uranus and the 7th house cusp. The rift between the United States and a few other countries may widen, and with Mars in the sky aligning with the United State's Pluto at 27 degrees of Capricorn, there could be greater military action and some stressful negotiations going on. Mars is also aligned with President Barack Obama's Saturn at 25 degrees of Capricorn, meaning he may be dealing with forces that are hard to control.

President Obama will also experience his Chiron Return on December 21, 2012, so there could be a life or death situation on his hands. According to the chart, on this day Saturn, at 8 degrees of Scorpio, conjuncts President Obama's Neptune. Under this transit, he will have terrific powers of concentration as he makes his decisions with a steady hand. Behind the scenes, however there will be activities that will not be documented and disclosed.

The Midheaven of the December 21st chart at 19 degrees of Sagittarius also conjuncts the Jupiter of North Korea's chart. That country could be involved with part of the world regeneration that is predicted at this time. Also, North Korea's Ceres at 27 degrees of Cancer opposes the United State's Pluto, involving a deep hurt that has evolved as an outcome of the Korean War. On this day, Mars will hit both of those points, possibly bringing about a surprise action.

The two solar eclipses in 2012 will be somewhat mild—and that gives us a hint that there will probably not be a huge catastrophe on Earth. The solar eclipse on May 20, 2012, at zero Gemini has the energy of success for many, and great scientific breakthroughs. The solar eclipse on November 13, 2012, at 22 degrees of Scorpio has a positive twist, and suggests many people are feeling joyful, with more pregnancies and births being reported.

The Maya were very conscious of the planet Venus. They went to war and planted crops according to various Venus transits. On June

8, 2004, transiting Venus eclipsed the Sun. There will be another eclipse of Venus and the Sun on June 6, 2012, completing the eight-year pairing of Venus/Sun Eclipses. These Venus transits happen once every one hundred years and foretell great changes. The last Venus Transit occurred in 1874 and 1882, which accelerated the Industrial Revolution. The next Venus Transit will occur in 2117 and 2125, suggesting a continuation of the techno-spiritual revolution. The Venus Transit is another astronomical phenomenon that precedes a great step of evolution on Earth.

> *The Venus Transit is another astronomical phenomenon that precedes a great step of evolution on Earth.*

At the time of this writing (October 2009), Saturn has been opposing Uranus. Saturn represents the old structure of society, and Uranus represents transformative pushes to eliminate old structures. Saturn exactly opposed Uranus on September 15, 2009, which marks another shift in our world situation. This happens again in late April of 2010 and once again in late July of 2010, when the world will begin to function in a fundamentally different way.

On October 28, 2011, using the calculations of the Mayan Calendar, the day will reflect the position of "13 Ahau." This means completion and keeping life simple. There will be media attention on that day as well. Prepare to live more frugally in the future. Mother Earth's resources are more fragile now, but I believe that into the next 5,125-year era she will be rescued and treated fairly.

Brenda Black, CAP, is a professional astrologer certified by ISAR (International Society for Astrological Research). A professional astrologer in Phoenix, Arizona, for over twenty-eight years, Brenda holds workshops and gatherings locally, and appears nationally at conferences and expos of both an astrological and spiritual nature. A focus of her work is using astrology, tarot, numerology and other psychic tools to counsel and guide baby boomers as they go through life changes.

Brenda is a scholar of the Mayan Calendar "Tzolkin" and appears weekly on her Internet radio show Your Astrology Now, *heard on www.AchieveRadio.com. She is the co-author of a book on astrology,* Revisioning Lilith, The Dark Goddess, *and publishes a monthly astrological newsletter,* News Notes. *Brenda has spent many years on the Board of Directors of the Arizona Society of Astrologers and gives workshops on the Mayan calendar and 2012. She has a Bachelor of Arts degree in Russian from the University of Washington in Seattle. To learn more about Brenda, visit www.AstrologyForBabyBoomers. com.*

Peter Russell

EPICENTER OF A
CULTURAL EARTHQUAKE

People come to me and say, "What do you think is going to happen on December 21, 2012?" And my response is, "Nothing much." There will probably be a lot of people throwing 2012 parties or holding vigils because they believe something awful is going to happen. But there's nothing in the Mayan calendar that says something will happen on that particular day, only that a 5,124-year cycle will be completed then. Whether there will actually be momentous changes in 2012, or on December 21, 2012, remains to be seen. Indeed, almost every prediction ever made related to a specific date has failed to materialize.

How long is a moment in history? Is it a second, a minute, a day, a year? A decade? For me, the exact date is not so important. Rather, I see 2012 as a symbol of a critical period in human history. The year 2012 sits in the middle of this period, a time when we will see major changes, major transformations of humanity—and perhaps even an awakening of the human spirit. Rather than as a precise date on which major changes happen, I see 2012 as the temporal epicenter of a cultural earthquake.

The key prefix, *epi*, means "near" or "surrounding." No exact center or source of an earthquake can be pinpointed; there is no village you can point to and say, "This is where it began." An earthquake is felt all around—and it's the same with 2012. We can already feel its vibrations. We can feel that things are getting shakier. Whether it's the economy, the environment or climate change, we're experiencing very rapid change and transformation. We're getting closer and closer to the epicenter of that change, and the closer we get the more we will feel its reverberations.

> *Meditation is an important tool to help us navigate these times.*

No one actually knows what will happen in the coming years, but I do think many people are aware that we cannot go on the way we have been on this planet. We may see breakdowns in systems, and major social disruptions. And we will also probably see some real breakthroughs, positive transformations and people letting go of old attitudes and beliefs. All that we can say with certainty is that there will be a lot more change, and some of it totally unexpected. So how do we meet these changes?

Meditation is an important tool to help us navigate these times. The rate of change in our lives is speeding up; this has been going on throughout history. Today, with digital communications, things move a lot faster than they did just a generation ago. As we move into the future, this acceleration will continue. Developments will come more and more rapidly, piling atop one another. Increasing change requires us to adapt faster and faster, and we're going to experience more pressure and more stress; the ability to stop, slow down, unwind and release tension will become more and more essential. Meditation is a very good way to unwind from stress. An inner quieting of the mind can provide healing benefits in many areas of life.

Meditation also helps us get in touch with who we really are and what we really want. Often we get caught up in what society expects of us, and we neglect to delve into our own deeper, inner truth. As things start changing faster, we're going to need that depth of inner stability in our lives. An analogy I often use is of a tree in a forest. In a storm, a tree needs strong roots if it's going to avoid being blown over. We will not experience just "winds of change" in this cultural epicenter of the cultural earthquake that includes 2012; we'll be feeling veritable *storms* of change.

So, how can we learn to cope with this storm of change? We too really need to have strong inner roots; to be more firmly anchored in ourselves; to know who we really are and what's important. That way, we can remain centered, a calm inside the storms of change. Meditation is a great tool for identifying and strengthening our inner roots.

Trees have a native wisdom: do we ever see them bending *against* the wind? They bend, but do not break, under the terrific pressure of violent storms. We too need to develop flexibility in order to meet these stormy times. What worked in the past may not work today, and if we remain intractable, we may break. Meditation increases our flexibility by enabling us to let go of some of our attachments to "how things should be." And that allows us to accept the present moment as it unfolds, rather than being caught up in, "This isn't what I think it should be!" Expectations can create a lot of tension.

> *A tree is much better off in a storm if it's part of a forest than if it's standing off on its own in a field.*

Developing compassion is another very important tool for helping us meet these challenging times. As change comes faster, we need to care more for other people, and for ourselves. We'll need to cultivate the ability to put ourselves in other people's shoes, to begin to understand how they feel and the changes they're going through. It's really going to be important to develop a stronger sense of community. A tree is much better off in a storm if it's part of a forest than if it's standing off on its own in a field.

Meditation leads us to the next great frontier, which is not outer space, but inner space. We humans have vast amounts of knowledge, but still very little wisdom. Buckminster Fuller called this time "our final evolutionary exam." Is our species fit to survive? Can we develop the wisdom to use our prodigious powers for our own good, and for that of generations to come? We have made amazing progress in understanding the world around us and how to manipulate it. Who knows, in five years, what we'll be able to create? We've almost become masters of the material world.

> *We've relieved ourselves of a lot of the external sources of suffering, discomfort and pain; if we still suffer it's because there's something internal that hasn't been looked at.*

But we still know very little about the world inside us. We probably don't know much more about it than people did in the time of the ancient Greeks. And yet our own minds and how they work is the most important area that we have yet to explore. What's going wrong in the world—whether it's sociological, economic or personal—all comes back to human thinking, actions, consciousness and decision-making. And yet we know so little about what determines our response to situations and the extent to which our feelings and past experience unconsciously come into play.

What do we actually mean by "self" in the first place? That's one of the greatest mysteries. What do we mean by "I?" Science is only beginning to move in this direction, to ask, "What is consciousness?" The more we can understand ourselves and why we behave and think the way we do, the more we can free ourselves. At the moment, we are firmly trapped in our thinking, attitudes and belief systems. We may have created a lot of external freedom—we can travel easily, and many of us have a lot of financial freedom—but our fear, anger, jealousy and hope can still trap us and lead us to suffering.

We've relieved ourselves of a lot of the external sources of suffering, discomfort and pain; if we still suffer it's because there's something internal that hasn't been looked at.

The message of this period that includes 2012 is that it's time for us to change, to become new and better human beings. That really only comes from our understanding ourselves better and finding greater freedom from the inner patterns that run us. The new human being is more in touch with the true self than the ego sense that's conditioned by society. We're conditioned to obsess about what other people think of us. We're conditioned to believe that if we only had the right things, the right experiences, if only people would relate to us in the right way, we'd be happy.

In this sense, we've sold ourselves out to the world around us. But the truth that many spiritual teachings point toward is that whether or not we're at peace inside doesn't depend so much on what we have or do, as on how we *relate* to what we have and how we see ourselves.

Deep inside, there is an inner contentment and satisfaction that's always there, even when things are changing in unexpected ways. If we can tap into that truth using meditation and other tools, and reconnect with that deep sense of peace and well-being, *that* is the essence of the transformation that we are being called to, the quality that will unite us as a forest grown strong to withstand the cultural earthquake.

Peter Russell coined the term "global brain" with his 1980s bestseller of the same name, in which he predicted the impact of the Internet. He is the author of ten other books, including Waking Up in Time *and* From Science to God, *and is the producer of two award-winning videos. He is also the producer and creator of a two-CD set of meditations called* The 2012 MindShift: Meditations for Times of Accelerating Change.

Peter holds degrees in theoretical physics, experimental psychology and computer science from the University of Cambridge, England. In India, he studied meditation and Eastern philosophy. In the 1970s, he pioneered the introduction of personal growth programs to corporations, running courses for senior management on creativity, stress management and sustainable development.

Peter's principal interest is the inner challenges of the times we are passing through. Until now, Western science has largely ignored the exploration of consciousness, leaving it to philosophers, mystics and sages. Peter believes that if we are to navigate our way safely through these turbulent times, we need to listen to the wisdom these people have accumulated over the centuries, as well as to our current scientific understanding. To learn more about Peter, visit www. PeterRussell.com.

SO WHAT IS THE NEXT STEP IN OUR JOURNEY?

It is my sincere desire that a spark of divine inspiration has called you to this book and toward a deeper exploration of a more expansive path. You are on the front lines of this amazing shift; this is your opportunity to participate in creating our positive future.

The esteemed authors in this book have offered an abundance of information, tools and resources to help you reach your full human potential. They have helped to chart a new direction, free from fear and uncertainty, toward harmony between people—and between nations. Now it is up to us to share this information with others and let our lives serve as an example of the type of world we could create together.

Though there has been focus on the date of December 21, 2012, there is also wide acknowledgment in the pages of this book that this shift is not about a specific date on the calendar, but rather is a process of paradigm change, of conscious shifting. This process began years ago, and we are currently approaching a peak of that shift. Now is the time to prepare for the change in consciousness, to evolve our lifestyles, to build and maintain supportive communities, and to begin living in harmony with the Earth and with one another.

There is also an acknowledgment in this book that the shift is not only in our culture and on our planet, but also in the deep resources of our spiritual being. As above, so below. All is connected, all is one.

Along with evolving your personal lifestyle, this shift is an opportunity to advance your spiritual understanding, connection and being. Now is the time to develop, fine-tune and follow your inner voice—the same voice that inspired you to pick up this book. You have unlimited opportunity to connect with spirit and live from your purpose, with flow and ease.

> *Now is the time to prepare for the change in consciousness, to evolve our lifestyles, to build and maintain supportive communities, and to begin living in harmony with the Earth and with one another.*

Transforming Through 2012, the first in a series of print books and online multi-media ebooks, is the beginning of a cutting-edge conversation about the evolving universe—the external universe and the one inside of us. In future books we will bring you esteemed authors, the leading visionaries and experts of our time, as we continue to explore the next steps in anchoring the new paradigm. Future themes may include: the emergence of the divine feminine; the new ecology; the new economy and survival on the new Earth; and super-health and spirituality.

I hope this book and future books in the series give you a greater understanding of 2012. My intention is to provide a platform for dialogue to help clear confusion and offer possibilities for co-creating our future, guided by wisdom and positive action. This is an amazing time. We are witnessing a powerful conscious shift filled with opportunities to share appreciation, blessings, wisdom—and most of all, love.

I look forward to joining you on the journey as we transform through 2012 with grace and ease, and through love.

Debra Giusti
April 2, 2010

ABOUT DEBRA GIUSTI

Debra Giusti has spent the last thirty years fulfilling her life's mission, creating a series of businesses that provide "transformational doorways" opening to vast hubs of cutting edge information and resources. Experienced by millions of people, the journey through these doorways offers a wealth of opportunities to transform oneself, the community and the planet, achieve greater health and harmony and assist humankind in anchoring the "new global paradigm." Through this 2012 Book Series she continues sharing her passionate support of the current consciousness shift.

In 1978, Debra founded the Harmony Festival in Santa Rosa, California, which has evolved into a three-day outdoor festival of music, art, ecology, health and spirituality. Attended by more than thirty-five-thousand people every June, the Harmony Festival features top entertainers and speakers as well as major attractions including the Eco Village, Wellness Pavillion, Goddess Grove, Healing Sanctuary and Sports Action Zone. In 1978, Debra also launched Wishing Well Distributing Co., which distributed more than three-thousand health and new age products and videos nationwide. She is also the founder of the Well Being Community Center and Newspaper in Sonoma County, California, the Spirit of Christmas Crafts Faire and Celebration, and other transformational events.

Debra is currently developing the online version of the Harmony Festival (www.HarmonyFestivalOnline.com), the Harmony Connections bimonthly e-Newsletter, and the next books in the *Transforming Through 2012* book series. To learn more about the book series visit www.TransformingThrough2012.com. To learn more about the Harmony Festival, visit www.HarmonyFestival.com. To learn more about Debra, visit www.DebraGiusti.com.

Resource Guide for the New Paradigm

Breakthrough Products • Movies • Art • Music

www.2012MultiMediaEbook.com
www.TransformingThrough2012.com

BREAKTHROUGH PRODUCTS

Quantumwave Lasers

The ScalarWave Laser is a revolutionary quantum device to unwind stress, tension, dis-ease, to activate biological processes and help shift into unity consciousness.

Stillpoint Now, Paul & Lillie Weisbart
www.quantumwavelasers.com

Amega Wand

AmWand is a futuristic tool created to resonate at zero point energy to help our bodies source the needed universal life force energy for better health.

Amega Global, Deborah Pozin
www.eamega.com/healthyu

Energetic Interactions

New standard, new paradigm. EI is the future of skin technology, the science of mathematical algorithms (codes) for cellular rejuvenation.

Energetic Interactions, Tara Grace
www.EnergeticInteractions.com/taragrace

Signals/Stem 120

Where biotech, infotech and nanotech meet to reverse aging by 2029.

Signals, Tara Grace
www.stem120.com

DOCUMENTARY FILMS

2012 and The Ascension Process

This site contains beautiful transformative music video programs and art designed to inspire, delight, heal and enlighten.

Artainment, DaVid Raphael, MD

www.Artainment.com

2012 The Odyssey & Time Wave 2013

Armageddon Is Not What It Used to Be and *The Future is Now* speak to the transformative nature of our times, and the critical issues we face.

Sacred Mysteries, Sharron Rose

www.SacredMysteries.com

Beyond 2012: Evolving Perspectives On The Next Age

Beyond 2012 presents a wide variety of evolving perspectives with techniques for social and ecological transformation.

UFO TV & Spirit Culture, Tim Crawford

www.UFOTV.com

Making the Quantum Leap

The first docudrama/comedy exploring personal and social transformation through quantum physics, consciousness and figure skating.

Continuum Center, Jane Barrash

www.ContinuumCenter.net

Metaphysia 2012

A remarkable vision quest of personal and planetary transformation, revealing the hidden metaphysical mysteries of 2012.

Sean M. Fisher, Writer/Director

www.Metaphysia2012.com

RESOURCE GUIDE FOR THE NEW PARADIGM

Return of The Ancestors

A film to empower humanity and shape our future. Nearly 100 elders from around the world joined together to bring the voices of our ancestors.

Institute for Cultural Awareness, Adam Yellowbird
www.ICA8.org

Quantum Communication

High quality definition films exploring the power of consciousness, human potential, enlightenment, quantum physics and ecology.

Voice Entertainment, David Sereda
www.VoiceEntertainment.net

What on Earth? Inside the Crop Circle Mystery

Full of wonder and mystery, this hauntingly beautiful film has been widely hailed as the best documentary on crop circles ever made!

Mighty Companions, Suzanne Taylor
www.CropCircleMovie.com

The Wiz Kidz

An inspiring children's program created to boost confidence and self-esteem. *The Secret* for kids—with songs & puppets!

Espavo Productions, Pamela Pedder
www.TheWizKidz.com

EDUCATIONAL AUDIO, BOOK, & VIDEOS

Sounds True

Explore Mysteryof2012.com, the authoritative guide by experts on Mayan prophecies. Free audio downloads and 2012 countdown widget.

www.Mysteryof2012.com

MUSIC & ART

2012: Ascension Harmonics

Sounds for transformation, vibrational activation, and frequency shifts! Visionary Award Winner for "Best Meditation/Healing Music"!

Jonathan Goldman Spirit Music

www.HealingSounds.com

Art Beyond Vision

Techno-mystic visual art in service to the next dimension of experience.

Android Jones

www.AndroidJones.com

Awakening the Divine

Aaron Pyne of Portland, OR, is a visionary artist, sacred graphic and web designer with a focus on spiritual, eco, & holistic businesses.

Visionary Artist, Graphic, & Web Designer, Aaron Pyne

www.SpiritAP.com

Davin Infinity

Freelance graphic design and video for the new Earth awakening.

Davin Infinity, Davin Skonberg

www.ShamanEyes.net

EMERGENCE: Beyond 2012?

The sacred geometry Paintings, *EMERGENCE: Beyond 2012?* film, DVD, T-shirts. New World flag, Divine Metaphysics 101, The Master Almanac.

David Alexander English

www.DavidAlexanderEnglish.com

Synergenesis Visionary Art & Healing Music

Music, art, seminars and sacred ceremonies for accessing multi-dimensional consciousness. Books, training manuals and videos on soul embodiment.

Synergenesis, Amoraea Dreamseed

www.SynergenesisCode.com